Deceit, Disappearance & Death
on Hilton Head Island

Deceit, Disappearance & Death
on Hilton Head Island

by
Charlie Ryan
With Pamela Martin Ovens

Single Star ★
A Division of Ovens Onboard, Ltd.
Hilton Head Island

★

Deceit, Disappearance & Death
on Hilton Head Island

First Published in 2018 by
Single Star
A Division of Ovens Onboard, Ltd.
Hilton Head Island

First Edition
Printed in the United States of America

For information or purchases contact:
Single Star, Publisher
PO Box 5566, Hilton Head Island, SC 29938
www.singlestar.us
sail@singlestar.us or 843-290-9900
Manufacturing by ArtBookPrinting.com
a specialty markets company of InnerWorkings, Inc.

Cover Design: Pamela Martin Ovens
Cover photograph: William L. Bosley
bosleyimages.com

Library of Congress Cataloging in Publication Data
Names: Ryan, Charlie & Ovens, Pamela Martin
Title: Deceit, Disappearance & Death on Hilton Head Island
About the disappearance of Elizabeth & John Calvert on Hilton Head Island
ISBN 978-0-9973290-7-0 (paperback)

We lovingly dedicate this book to
Amalfi, Rosencrantz & Guildenstern

Contents

Introduction by the Authors

The inspiration for this book was a desire to comprehensively chronicle the mysterious disappearance of Hilton Head Island's John and Elizabeth Calvert and the death of their accountant, Dennis Gerwing.

To commemorate the 10th Anniversary of the case that burst open March 3, 2008, we reviewed and organized thousands of previous details of the Calvert investigation and added extensive new detail to a criminal case that remains open to this day.

In our pursuit, we interviewed numerous islanders and others who were employed by the Calverts, knew them socially, were related to them or provided professional services to them. We performed the same exercises in regard to Dennis Gerwing's supposed suicide. We also interviewed Beaufort County Sheriff P.J. Tanner, his Lead Investigator Angela Viens and Detective Bob Bromage, as well as reporters who covered the story.

We filed a Freedom of Information Act (FOIA) request with the Beaufort County Sheriff's Office and the FOIA was readily provided to us. So far as we know, ours is the only FOIA filed in the Calvert case, and, at the time we received the material, it had been seen only by investigative authorities.

The FOIA contained more than 600 pages. We carefully reviewed each of those pages, and from them we have presented considerable new information in the Calvert case. We also gathered and reviewed a decade of voluminous newspaper, magazine, broadcast and social media articles that were dedicated to the story as it advanced through the years.

We believe this compilation of materials is the most complete public accounting of the mysterious disappearance of John and Elizabeth Calvert, and the controversial death of Dennis Gerwing. But, opinions still differ. Broadly speaking, two theories remain as to what happened on March 3, 2008 at the offices of The Club Group at Sea Pines Center. One segment strongly believes Dennis Gerwing murdered the Calverts in his office, disposed of the bodies, and, a few days later, committed suicide—case closed.

A second faction remains convinced, beyond doubt, that Gerwing did not act alone—that others aided him in killing the Calverts; they believe Gerwing was then violently killed by criminal elements who staged his death as a suicide.

Ten years of debate have provided no solid answers, but we hope our research into the Hilton Head Island's most interesting mystery will some day be of assistance in solving the Calvert case.

Note the FOIA information is quoted verbatim and sometimes there are grammatical errors. We tried to put this information in italics for ease of reading the material.

If you have relevant information regarding this case, please call the Beaufort County Sheriff's Office at 1·888·CRIMESC.

"They were here, and then they weren't. It was as if someone had airbrushed them right off the landscape of their lives."

Sean Morgan

"There's this nag in your heart that says while we don't know what has happened to them, it is more that we don't know where they are."

David White

"Words, however, don't cause the deepest sting. Worse is the fear that someone might get away with a horrible crime against two good people. But before there can be justice, there must be answers. Friends hope that ship hasn't sailed."

Tom Barton

"I think Dennis lost his moral compass when his mother died."

Fred Gerwing

"Cab services and taxis in Hilton Head didn't pick anyone up. That would lead anyone to believe that there was a second party, which very well could be. You just hope someone with some loyalty to Dennis Gerwing at some point will decide, 'OK, well, he's dead.'"

Sheriff P.J. Tanner

Chapter 1

★

They Are Missing

"Whatever has happened to them, you've got to put them to rest," said David White in a memorial service for his sister Elizabeth Calvert and her husband John on November 15, 2009, in Atlanta, Georgia—20 months after their mysterious disappearance on Hilton Head Island, South Carolina's playground paradise.

The prominent couple vanished March 3, 2008, without a trace, and ten years later Hilton Head's biggest mystery remains unsolved. Were the Calverts murdered? Was it a professional "hit"? Were they alive and in a witness protection program? And, what about the "suicide" of Dennis Gerwing, a trusted adviser to the Calverts? It was the most unusual suicide forensic experts had ever seen, or so they said.

It was a storybook life—the Calverts owned an elegant home in Atlanta and a second home in Savannah, GA. John lived on Hilton Head full time aboard the Calvert's 40-foot Hatteras yacht, *Yellow Jacket*, and Liz Calvert split her week between Harbour Town and Savannah where she practiced law with a prestigious firm.

The Calverts were high-end entrepreneurs. They owned or ran several businesses on Hilton Head, including the Harbour Town Yacht Basin, Harbour Town Power Boats, and Harbour Town Resorts.

Their companies were marquee in the almost 5000-acre Sea Pines Plantation where they and their employees managed 125 rental properties, the marina slips, numerous fishing charters, yacht and fuel services, water sports activities and sightseeing cruises. The Calverts were involved in the community. They were considered to be stellar additions to the island.

Then came March 4, 2008, and everything changed.

At 6:40 pm that day, Nancy Cappelmann, the harbourmaster at the Harbour Town Yacht Basin, reported to the Beaufort County Sheriff's Office that her employers, John and Elizabeth Calvert, were missing. After Nancy notified him, David White made a similar call to law enforcement in Atlanta, saying that his sister and brother-in-law were last seen the prior day on the 12-mile long barrier island known as Hilton Head, just across the Intracoastal Waterway from Bluffton, SC.

White had gone to his sister's residence in Atlanta and gained access to the house, but his sister and brother-in-law were not there.

Pressed as to why they thought the Calverts were missing, rather than out-of-pocket or traveling, both Cappelmann and White said it was uncharacteristic for them not to show up for business meetings they had scheduled. The Beaufort County Sheriff's Office received the call with routine interest, as did authorities in Atlanta—they thought there was little cause for alarm.

Reports of missing persons were somewhat commonplace in resort communities and usually ended with the "missing" showing up a day or so later. However, the Sheriff's Office gladly went through its normal procedure, assuring Cappelmann it would list the Calverts as missing that very night. True to the office's word, both John and Elizabeth were entered into the National Crime Information Center (NCIC) as entry numbers M617250342 and MO57217633,

2

respectively.

March 5, 2008 dawned without a trace of the Calverts. Sheriff P.J. Tanner dispatched an investigator to Hilton Head and Harbour Town with instructions to begin questioning John and Elizabeth Calvert's associates as to when they had last seen their employers.

Officer Tony Serrato crossed the Intracoastal Waterway to Hilton Head Island. He formulated questions about the reported disappearance as he drove to Sea Pines Plantation at the southern end of the island. The investigator would not be alone—Sheriff Tanner would eventually assign multiple detectives to investigate the Calvert case.

At the Harbour Town Yacht Basin, Harbourmaster Cappelmann met with Serrato. She again said that she had become concerned when John Calvert had not shown up for a meeting the afternoon of March 4. She fretted, "John is never late, so when 20 minutes went by, I got worried and called his cell, but it went straight to voicemail like it was turned off."

Cappelmann told officer Serrato she arrived at her marina office the morning of March 4 to find the lights had been left on from the night before—that never happened. She then found John's briefcase on the floor in a common area of the office. Strange—she had never seen John's briefcase left unattended. That was odd, she thought. Then, she found files in her office that Elizabeth had planned to take to a meeting on March 3, the night prior, with Dennis Gerwing, the CFO for The Club Group, who handled financial affairs for the Calvert businesses.

Chapter 2

The Search Begins

Investigator Serrato made copious notes as Nancy Cappelmann recounted further details of March 4. She had asked Leslie Whitener to walk around the Yacht Basin to the Calvert yacht, *Yellow Jacket*, and see if the Calverts were there. The employee was back within the hour to report that she had called out, asking if anyone was aboard, and received no reply. She told Nancy she had boarded the boat and looked around, but saw no one.

She did, however, encounter "TC", the Calvert's cat. TC was short for "The Cat". Both TC and Sadie, the Calvert's dog, lived on the boat. A search for Sadie proved fruitless. Sadie was nowhere to be seen.

The whole thing was strange, Nancy said if her bosses went out of town they always asked her to care for TC. But, TC had been left unattended. Nancy knew of no travel plans the Calverts may have had. Surely, they would have informed her if they were going to travel. They always did that.

Nancy's worries became deeper. She got into her car to make an extensive inspection of all the parking lots in Harbour Town—looking for John Calvert's vehicle. Her search was futile; his car was not on any of the lots. At that point, she wondered, could the Calverts have had a major automobile accident? She decided to call Liz Calvert's Savannah law office. She placed the call and asked for the cell phone number of Liz's brother David White.

In Atlanta, David was just leaving work when his cell phone rang. It was Nancy, asking him to call his sister because she and John seemed to be missing. He said later, "I thought, "Oh, no worries, I'll give them a call," never imagining that he would never see or hear from his sister and brother-in-law again.

Nancy hesitated. She looked at the investigator and wondered if she should bring up one last thought. She plowed ahead, adding that one more thing—something, she said, "that got his interest."

She said she knew the Calverts were scheduled to meet late on March 3 with Dennis Gerwing of The Club Group, a company that helped manage the Calvert's business affairs. Nancy told Serrato that the purpose of the meeting was Liz's concerns that there were improprieties in the Calvert companies' accounting reports—reports that were the sole responsibility of Dennis Gerwing.

So far as anyone knew, no one had seen Liz and John since the evening of March 3.

Gerwing was the Chief Financial Officer for The Club Group. The property management company not only managed Sea Pines Center, the shopping mall inside Sea Pines Plantation where The Club Group offices were located, it also handled many of the Calvert's business affairs, including leasing and accounting services. Gerwing was not new to the task—he had managed finances for 20 years for the companies the Calverts had purchased, working for the folks who previously owned the operations.

It was logical, some said, that the Calverts continued the practice of farming out to The Club Group some of the management of their holdings. Dennis Gerwing would be responsible for the financial segment of the arrangement. "That's not unusual," Tom Gardo of Denarius Group, Inc. was quoted as saying, "it's a pretty common type of thing." Liz had said she knew the arrangement would cost a little more money at first, but it would be money well spent to get up to speed quickly.

Chapter 3

★

"Oh, Great!"

Nancy Cappelmann knew of the Calvert's Club Group arrangement and, the fact was, she told investigators, she had called Dennis Gerwing when she feared the Calverts were missing. She had decided she was going to let the conversation determine if Dennis had seen them, but Dennis did not pick up—all she got was his answering machine.

Around noon Dennis called Harbour Town Yacht Basin and talked with Leslie Whitener, an associate of Nancy's. He wanted a weather forecast. Leslie was known to be the Yacht Basin's most accurate forecaster of weather—she was called the "Weather Wizard".

Nancy motioned to Leslie; she wanted to speak with Dennis.

"I was reluctant to ask him about John because I just didn't want him to know that I did not have any idea where John was," Nancy said. "Have you talked to John today?" Nancy asked Dennis.

"I haven't. I know Liz is working in Savannah Monday and Tuesday," Gerwing replied. Nancy said later she was pretty sure Dennis had said during the conversation that he and Liz had last met on Sunday, March 2 and again March 3.

"Before the end of the day, Tuesday, March 4, 5:00 pm or so, Dennis called again to see if anyone had heard from John and Liz. I was getting pretty frantic by then, and I told him I was going to call Sea Pines Security Chief George Breed," Nancy recounted.

The next day, March 5, Dennis called Nancy again, this time early in the morning.

"Has anyone heard from John and Liz?" Dennis asked.

Nancy replied that she had filed a missing persons report and had told the Sheriff's Office about accounting irregularities of which Liz was suspicious.

"He didn't seem very concerned about that, but he did seem genuinely concerned that no one had heard from John and Liz," she said.

Later that day Nancy boarded the *Yellow Jacket*, looking for records of the Calvert's credit card numbers and account information.

"There was a message on my cell phone. It was Dennis, suggesting we look at the airports for their cars," Nancy said.

She again talked with Dennis after he left a message concerning resort issues. She returned his call and told him she had just left the Sheriff's Office, having given them more information.

"Dennis, I told them you were the last person to have seen John and Liz," Nancy said.

"Oh, great," Dennis uttered.

"I don't remember if I told him that the Sheriff's Office wanted to talk with him, or if he asked," Nancy said. She then gave him the number at the Beaufort County Sheriff's Office, and he said he would call. "That was the last conversation I had with him," she said.

Investigator Serrato took in all the nuances, made his notes and concluded his interview. He then asked Harbourmaster Cappelmann to take him to *Yellow Jacket*. There, forensic associates joined him, and they searched the boat from stem to stern. Nothing appeared out of order, and there were no signs of a struggle—the *Yellow Jacket* was ship-shape.

On March 6, the Beaufort County Sheriff's Office lead investigator Sergeant Angela Viens also chatted with Nancy Cappelman. Viens' record of the conversation is in the FOIA obtained by the authors on August 10, 2017.

Inv. Novak and I went to Harbour Town Marina and met with Nancy Cappelman on 03-06-08. Cappelman allowed us access to the Calvert's boat (Yellow Jacket) that was docked at Harbour Town. I photographed the boat. I noted that there were clothes hanging behind the door in the bedroom. Cappelman indicated that those were the clothes that Elizabeth Calvert wore to work on 03-03-08. I collected several personal items from the boat in an effort to obtain a DNA profile for John and Elizabeth Calvert. I collected a Harbour Town coffee cup, a water bottle, an electric toothbrush and two hair brushes. I also collected two black binders and a Sony VAIO computer. Cappelman indicated that she believed they were possibly missing John's computer. The boat appeared in order. There were no signs of struggle inside of the boat and nothing appeared out of ordinary or suspicious. The compartments within the boat were also checked.

We then went to John and Elizabeth Calvert's office. Cappelman indicated that Elizabeth had thoroughly researched the financial information provided to them by The Club Group and had prepared reports based on what she was researching and had discovered. She said that the information that she collected was stored in binders in a locked closet in her office. Cappelman provided us with 12 black binders, an external hard drive/computer accessory and a stack of bank statements from the closet. Cappelman indicated that the Calverts used their Discover Card almost exclusively and

they did not carry a lot of cash. I obtained a signed receipt for property.
Those items were turned over to S/A Don DeMay of the FBI on 03-06-08
for review and analysis.

The yacht searches ended at about the same time that Dekalb County, GA law officials gained access to the Calvert's elegant home in Atlanta and began a search from top to bottom. They found the Calvert's Porsche and their white truck, but there was no one at home, and nothing untoward was discovered in the house.

There *was* something odd—the Calvert's Atlanta neighbor, Goodloe H. Yancey III, was quoted as saying a light was on in the Calvert home. Yancey said that was rare when the Calverts were away.

Investigators called Elizabeth Calvert's law offices, Hunter Maclean in Savannah, and talked with Liz's co-worker, Sally Nielsen. She told them Liz had not shown up for work and that she had not been able to contact her. Echoing Nancy Cappelmann, Nielsen said Liz had told her several times she suspected an embezzlement problem with an outside accounting firm regarding the Harbour Town accounts.

In 2013, five years after Nancy Cappelmann reported the Calverts missing, Sean Morgan of the newspaper, *Bluffton Today*, wrote, "If there had been a soundtrack of their disappearance, it might have been the soft sound of an air lock closing, followed immediately by the cold silence of empty space occupied. They were here, and then they weren't. It was as if someone had airbrushed them right off the landscape of their lives."

Chapter 4

★

The Club Group

The Club Group, where Dennis was a partner, was founded in 1986, when Ginn Holdings of Hilton Head, which owned Sea Pines Resort and several other Hilton Head properties, was in danger of bankruptcy. Mark King and Dennis Gerwing, aware of the looming Ginn problems, decided to form The Club Group.

Silver-haired Mark King was from Pinehurst, NC and some referred to him as, "the fair-haired boy." He had a ready smile and southern drawl. He was an islander of good standing. He was close to Hilton Head icon and Sea Pines founder Charles Fraser and could entertain for hours about his many moments with Fraser, as King probed the developer's mind for why he did this or that, when bringing Hilton Head from an isolated jungle to an American playground—learning from the master.

Mark King and Dennis Gerwing had great respect for one another. They were both gentlemen and were considered the elite standard that Islanders hoped to achieve as the norm of island business and character. But, when Dennis fell upon hard times, one journalist felt Mark did not offer his full support to Dennis.

Savannah Morning News editorial page editor Tom Barton wrote in a 2008 column, "Friends said that Elizabeth Calvert, a sharp-eyed attorney for Savannah's largest law firm, Hunter Maclean, found Gerwing was cooking their books."

Barton continued, "Their claim would gain credibility on April 22, 2008, when Mark King, Gerwing's friend of 22 years and president of The Club Group, painted his buddy as a crook. That's when a forensic audit, initiated by the company, accused Gerwing of embezzling $2.1 million from the Calverts and seven other clients."

Others who knew both Gerwing and King strongly disagreed with that sentiment, knowing King was devastated that Dennis Gerwing might have been guilty of embezzling. His associates at The Club Group were universally supportive of King, as were those who knew him socially and in business.

Chapter 5

The Media Descends

The first media foray into Harbour Town following reports of the disappearance of prominent residents John and Liz Calvert was by two young reporters who would be in the vanguard of chronicling the strange island events in the first months of 2008.

Island Packet reporters Dan Brownstein and Tim Donnelly were journalists with advanced degrees in their field. Donnelly had a BA in Journalism from the University of Maryland, and Journalism and Philosophy degrees from George Washington University. Brownstein had graduated from Otterbein College with a BA in Communications and Broadcasting and had earned his Master in Business Administration from the University of South Carolina.

They were well-armed to take on a major story.

But, they had never encountered a humongous, stop the presses, news flash, special bulletin, gorilla size news blast such as the Calvert story.

Brownstein said, "It was probably the highlight of my time on Hilton

Head Island. Everyone was talking; the interest was so intense, we woke up each day with absolutely no clue what the story would be the following morning. It filled us with adrenaline. We felt terrible that these things had happened to people, but it was a great time to be a reporter."

Donnelly and Brownstein might have been young, but they were not the least bit hesitant to immediately put their noses to the ground and begin to investigate. Donnelly was no stranger to gossip on the island and had seen a few things. He reported in a story in the *Packet* on August 26, 2007, "If you've been on Hilton Head for a few years, you've probably heard some pretty potent rumors."

Donnelly's story quoted island gossip that Brad Pitt and Angelina Jolie had purchased a home in Wexford, that Oprah Winfrey was buying a house on Brams Point or Daufuskie Island, and a bartender at a local restaurant had slipped drugs into the drinks of a number of women, resulting in several deaths, followed by the bartender's suicide. Oh, and what about the rumors that Lindsay Lohan was in a rehab center in Shipyard?

All false.

Donnelly went so far as to do in-depth research on rumors and what caused them. An expert on the subject told him, "The need to share juicy news is high, especially in a small town like Hilton Head. There is a degree of collegiality that comes with gossiping with people you know. People feel connected and bonded."

Tim Donnelly rushed to Sea Pines following initial calls to *Packet* editors that said something major was afoot at Harbour Town. Donnelly had some doubt in his mind that the latest rumor—two high profile people were missing—was for real. Was this just more juicy "bonding" in a small town?

Donnelly passed through a security gate at the exclusive planta- tion and drove directly to Harbour Town. There, he parked his car, climbed out, slammed the door and began to ask questions of anyone he encountered at the Yacht Basin.

"Everyone was skittish, people were on edge, and I could sense this was something more than just a missing person thing," Donnelly said. After a few jousts with locals, he soon realized that people would say little this early in a possible criminal case. He abandoned his random interviewing encounters and headed directly for the yacht *Yellow Jacket*. Donnelly knew the Calverts lived on the boat when on Hilton Head Island.

The Calvert yacht was docked on the far side of the Basin in slip 83. Donnelly hurried there and drew up dockside, shouting, "Is anyone home?" There was no reply. Tim paced back and forth along the dock, leaning toward the boat, trying to peer into its windows.

With no one answering his calls, he climbed aboard and began to look around. He again peered through windows and noticed a light was on in the cabin. He put his ear to the cabin door and heard a muffled noise from what he thought was either a radio or television broadcast. He knocked on the cabin door and again asked in a loud voice if anyone was aboard.

"I got no response, and then I saw a newspaper at the helm. I walked over and picked up the paper, and I opened the wrapper. Inside was that morning's edition of the *Island Packet*," Donnelly recalled.

Just then a patrol boat pulled alongside *Yellow Jacket* and an officer shouted at Tim, "Can I help you?"

Donnelly moved to the dock and said, "I'm looking for John and Elizabeth Calvert, do you know what happened to them?"

"The fellow just sort of turned his head and motored away," Tim recalled.

Not to be put off, the *Packet* reporter retraced his steps around the

Yacht Basin and entered the marina office. He asked if anyone knew anything about the Calverts.

"I was stonewalled," Donnelly said, "they deflected my questions and then threatened to call the police on me. I told them to stop bullshitting me and tell me what's going on."

Harbourmaster Nancy Cappelmann took charge and asked Donnelly to step outside. She said the Calverts were missing, that the Beaufort County Sheriff's Office had been contacted and that they were very worried. Donnelly called Dan Brownstein and Jim Faber at the *Packet* offices to relay details—they had, potentially, a big story on their hands.

"We were careful—lots of missing person cases go awry. This case was high profile, but we didn't, at first, want to make too much of a deal of it. Sometimes missing people show up the next day," Brownstein said.

Brownstein called the Beaufort County Sheriff's Office and spoke with Captain Toby McSwain who was responsible for security for the Hilton Head Island area of Beaufort County. "I asked Toby if the Calverts were missing and he said there was a meeting 'right now' where that very thing was being discussed. He said he had been hoping that we were not calling about the Calverts. The Sheriff's office was trying to keep a lid on the case until they could sort everything out. It became, very quickly, a dramatic story," Brownstein said.

The journalistic groundwork was exhaustive. Brownstein and Donnelly would find, in the weeks ahead, that the national media sought them out as the two most learned reporters on the case and they were often followed by a string of big TV names. They loved the job.

Donnelly and Brownstein were everywhere as they chased the story. There was an intense interest in the mystery at every level. Details— the public wanted details.

Brownstein and Donnelley would deliver.

Chapter 6

★

Grease Is The Word

O n March 5, 2008, the sun shone brightly, and the temperature climbed to only 68 degrees—and still no word from the Calverts whose names were now officially listed in the National Crime Information Center (NCIC) as missing persons. There was a mounting concern as their businesses went untended and employees sought direction. Something was amiss—the Calverts were very responsible people and, as Nancy Cappelmann had pointed out, John Calvert had missed a scheduled meeting to discuss promotions and budgeting for the marina's upcoming spring season.

John Calvert missing a meeting? That never happened.

"When I came out at 11:30 that morning, their boat looked undisturbed, and we wondered if they'd just slept in," said Tony Gibbus, who worked with the Calverts. "He's never missed a meeting," Gibbus said of Calvert, "and he's never turned off his cell phone. They would never just run off."

Sea Pines resident Patty Crews shook her head and said, "People are upset, losing sleep. It's so out of character for a peaceful Harbour

Town." An employee at Sea Pines Realty told local media, "Probably every hour, you hear a different story."

Across the Yacht Basin, near the Liberty Oak, Crazy Crab Restaurant's Marty Pellicci took a break from prepping for the evening crowd and told reporters, "We just keep hope that somehow, something positive can happen, even though it doesn't look good. We're just keeping our fingers crossed and praying, so, hopefully, we'll find something out soon, now that this situation has happened."

John and Elizabeth Calvert ate lunch and dinner quite often at the Crazy Crab. At times, they dined there every day of the week and regularly watched a game show on television with Pellicci. "They just loved it," a friend said of the Calverts' affection for the harbourside restaurant.

Dennis Gerwing also frequented the Crazy Crab. Bartender Chris Wagner said of the Calverts, "As nice a couple as you could hope to find." But, Wagner felt differently about Dennis Gerwing. "If you had money, he liked to talk with you. But, if you were just a regular bartender or waitress, he wouldn't give you the time of day."

Lynn Gamble, who took water sports reservations at Harbour Town, told the Associated Press, "If Liz is out walking her dog on a Saturday morning, she'll come in here and just sit and talk, shooting the breeze." As Gamble spoke from the harbourmaster's office, she looked out on the Calvert's yacht and said of Liz, "She's a down-to-earth, wonderful woman." Marina dockhand Abbie Adams chimed in, saying it wasn't unusual for the Calverts to join her and other employees for a cold beer after work.

Indeed, the Calverts were known for almost compulsively keeping in touch with the men and women who worked for their businesses. One employee said of the Calverts that they knew when their employees ate, slept or drank.

Larry Naylor, who docked his boat next to the Calvert's yacht, said he was aware that the chances of finding the Calverts alive were fading. "People don't know what to think," he said, "it's a very strange event." Throughout the investigation, so-called informants peppered the Beaufort County Sheriff's Office on a regular basis—look for the bodies here, look for them there. So, it was not unusual that an anonymous phone call was received that said, in a conspiratorial manner, that detectives should check out the grease trap at the Quarterdeck Restaurant at Harbour Town. There, deep in grease, they would find the bodies of John and Elizabeth Calvert. The caller, a male, said the grease trap was large enough to hold two bodies.

"Check it out," was the official order from the Sheriff's Office.

Tony Whiddon, facility maintenance manager for the Quarterdeck, fielded the call from the authorities.

"Can you drain it?" the Sheriff's Office asked.

Whiddon responded in the affirmative. A time and date were agreed upon for a meeting at the Quarterdeck—and the inspection and draining of the grease trap.

There, not quite believing it had come to this, Sheriff's Office investigators and Whiddon talked to Degler Waste Services.

The grease trap was located, opened and inspected before the draining. Nothing suspicious was observed, and Degler Waste Services began to drain the 500-gallon capacity grease trap.

It was much ado about nothing. Once draining was completed, the interior of the trap was inspected from top to bottom. Nothing was found, other than grease, and another "tip" was put to rest.
The Sheriff's Office was covering all bases—even if the base was covered in grease.

Meanwhile, the Calvert's cat, TC, was roaming the *Yellow Jacket*—abandoned, lonely, and waiting.

Chapter 7

Gerwing Faces Investigators

The Sheriff's Office was growing increasingly concerned. Investigators agreed they needed to talk to this fellow Dennis Gerwing.

From the FOIA, a "Supplemental Report" certified to be "true and correct" by Beaufort County Sheriff's Office Chief Deputy Michael M. Hatfield, states that "Corporal Meredith Florencio and Corporal Louis Novak were assigned to conduct a follow-up investigation into the Missing Persons report. Inv. Florencio and Inv. Novak conducted preliminary interviews on 03-04-08, including an interview with Dennis Gerwing."

The investigators met Dennis Gerwing in the reception area of The Club Group. Gerwing welcomed the two and immediately expressed his concern about the Calverts. He invited the investigators to his office, located at the rear of the suite of offices, where a door led outside to a two-story cement staircase. Dennis settled into his desk chair and invited Florencio and Novak to sit, and said he was certainly glad to answer any questions they might have.

It was the office in which Gerwing had met with the Calverts on

March 3. The furnishings were fairly austere.

Dennis chatted amiably with Florencio and Novak, and the meeting was cordial. There was one thing, however—Florencio noticed a laceration in the web of Gerwing's right hand.

"I noted he had two cuts on the web of his right hand. I asked him about the cut, and he advised me he cut himself on a wine bottle," Florencio wrote in her report of the meeting.

"John called me approximately two weeks ago and wanted to meet. He had questions regarding the Yacht Basin's and Resort's accounting functions," Gerwing said.

The investigators listened intently as Dennis related that he met with John Calvert on Sunday, February 16, where John inquired about a boat slip assessment that had been unpaid. "Gerwing said that he was surprised because Nancy (Cappelmann) always checks the accounts. He stated that he advised John that he would look into the issue and speak to his controller, Chris Martin," a report said.

Gerwing said that Liz continued to have questions regarding multiple accounting transfers that she did not understand.

To clear things up and eliminate all that suspicion, Gerwing met a second time with John and Elizabeth on February 24, 2008, regarding details of the "transfer of services" the Calverts had requested. Gerwing told Liz he felt the list of discrepancies she was concerned about was growing smaller.

Gerwing's accounting of the February 24 meeting aside, it is believed the Calverts angrily confronted Gerwing, claiming he had mismanaged more than $100,000 of their money. Little did they know other entities that Gerwing managed financially would also find "inconsistencies"—and that the total missing funds of all involved parties who trusted Dennis Gerwing would grow to a number far beyond $100,000.

Ellie "Titus", who told investigators that she was a very good friend of Elizabeth Calvert's, was privy to the Calvert's concern. She told authorities that Elizabeth felt at the end of December 2007, that the sum they were missing was large. Elizabeth, she said, wanted to research the situation a little bit more to find out how much money was missing. Titus told investigators she personally thought The Club Group was a front for some other enterprise because the marina and golf courses were not making money. Titus had lunch with Liz on March 3, 2008, the day the Calverts disappeared.

Leslie Whitener, who worked in the marina office and also was a very close friend of the Calverts, told investigators that suspicions were raised sometime around November 2007 when the Calverts began getting calls from creditors. One item was an unpaid bill for 10,000 gallons of gasoline.

Some who knew Liz Calvert described her as a "bulldog", and people knew that Gerwing did not like her. Little wonder—Elizabeth was demanding a full explanation of escrows, boat slip assessments, etc., and was making no secret of the fact she was convinced that she and John had been swindled by Gerwing. Dennis told Liz that he could explain any problems. "There's a computer glitch," he assured her, advising her not to worry. John Calvert repeated the phrase to Liz, telling her there was a software glitch at The Club Group. Liz replied, "Computers don't lose money."

Gerwing's feelings about Elizabeth grew even more cynical as she pressed ever harder for an explanation. At 5:10 pm on February 24, following his meeting with Elizabeth and John, he wrote an email to Laura Merrill that said, "Hi, just finished a meeting w/ the "Viper (Liz)" and came out on top…that's what the ole [sic] ego needed!!!"

Beaufort County Sheriff P.J. Tanner later seemed to agree that Elizabeth felt that Gerwing was stealing. "Elizabeth was convinced there was a problem. Dennis did not like Elizabeth. There was tension between those two, and he knew it," Tanner said.

With questions and stress still hanging in the air, Gerwing told investigators he requested a third meeting with both Calverts again present so that he could collectively provide answers to any continuing questions they might have. Florencio and Novak would question Dennis again the same afternoon at his home.

Chapter 8

★

Here—And Gone

On Monday, March 3, 2008, the temperature climbed to a mild 78° on Hilton Head Island and dropped that night to 68°. Skies were clear, there was no rain in the forecast, and the humidity was 66%. All in all, it was a lovely day weather-wise.

Video recordings documented that Elizabeth Calvert passed through Hilton Head Island's Cross Island Parkway toll plaza on March 3 at 5:32 pm. She was seen boarding the *Yellow Jacket* around 5:40. There, she changed into more casual clothing and hung her work attire in the closet.

Leaving the yacht, she donned dark glasses as the evening sun began to glisten off the waters of Calibogue Sound. She hurried across the coquina shell path that circled the Yacht Basin, hearing the pleasant sound of shells crunching beneath her feet. She crossed the parking lot and, it is assumed, went to her Mini Cooper and got in the car, exiting Harbour Town onto Lighthouse Road, and driving the short distance to Sea Pines Center for the scheduled meeting with Dennis Gerwing and her husband John.

"When did John Calvert arrive for the March 3 meeting?" investigators Florencio and Novak asked Dennis Gerwing.

"At 6:00 pm," Gerwing replied.

"And Elizabeth?"

"Elizabeth came separately, and walked through the door around 6:15," Gerwing said.

"How long was the meeting?"asked one of the investigators.

"About 15 minutes," was the reply.

Oddly enough, Gerwing said none of the issues that Elizabeth brought up the day before were discussed during the short meeting. The "computer glitch" was not discussed—or so Dennis Gerwing said.

"I was glad John arrived 15 minutes before Liz," Gerwing said. He was happy to have some time alone with John.

"I felt Liz did not know about a lot of the issues I had addressed with John. A lot of those problems were the root of the financial questions Liz was inquiring about," Gerwing said.

He told Florencio and Novak, "When Liz is around John, she is very passive, but by herself, dealing with these financial questions, she is very adamant."

When Liz arrived for the meeting, Gerwing said, "She appeared to be glazed over."

"She looked at her watch at 6:30," Dennis told the investigators. "She said, (to John) 'C'mon, we gotta' go," Dennis added, noting that she and John left together and, he assumed, went to dinner.

No witnesses saw the two leave The Club Group offices.

Chapter 9

The Long Road Home

Dennis Gerwing said he remained at The Club Group for another ten minutes following the Calvert's departure on March 3, and then he left, walking down the steps at Sea Pines Center and exiting the complement of shops into the front parking lot.

He walked towards the far end of the lot; Dennis said he always parked where his vehicle would not be subject to dents from negligent drivers who opened their car doors with abandon, damaging nearby cars. As Dennis made the trek to his Yukon, he saw Elizabeth's Mini Cooper near his Yukon—or, so he said.

But, there were different stories about that Mini Cooper—Nancy Cappelmann told investigators that she found Elizabeth's Mini Cooper in the Liberty Oak parking lot in Harbour Town on March 4, 2008, the day after the Calverts disappeared.

Dennis would say later that he left Sea Pines Plantation, wound through the Sea Pines Circle and exited onto US 278 William Hilton Parkway Business Route, passing Shipyard and Palmetto Dunes, taking the long route toward Hilton Head Plantation and home. Looking to gas up and buy a few lottery tickets, he said he pulled into Station One Convenience Store at 7:39 pm, choosing pump number 7. Dennis watched the pump numbers roll by as he gassed up—they stopped when they reached $52.46.

Tank full, he walked into the convenience store. He was wearing a yellow polo shirt with a Sea Pines logo. He stood at the convenience store register, repeatedly rubbing his hands and fingers together.

Dennis purchased a lottery ticket and left the store.

In the summary statistics that Dennis gave to investigators, he said he drove into Hilton Head Plantation and parked in his driveway at 8 Bent Tree Lane. He got out of the Yukon, pressed the lock switch on his key and walked to his house, unlocking the door and entering. Dennis prepared dinner—a special diet meal and drank some wine. He dropped the wine bottle. It broke. Dennis bent to clean up the broken glass, or so he said.

It was then, he later told Investigator Meredith Florencio, that he cut his hand on the broken wine bottle.

"How can you drink wine if you are on a diet?" Florencio asked.

"On my diet, you can drink wine," Dennis answered.

Dennis said at around 10:00 the same evening; he decided to return to The Club Group. This time he chose to drive his second vehicle, a Toyota Avalon. He stopped at the CVS pharmacy on the island's south end and bought Band-Aids for his cut hand. He then drove on to his office.

"I stayed at The Club Group until about midnight and then went home. I used the Cross Island Parkway back to Squire Pope Road and the back entrance to Hilton Head Plantation," Gerwing, told investigators.

It was a full day for Dennis Gerwing, and he soon retired for the evening, as March 3, 2008 came to a close and night winds drifted across Hilton Head Island.

Dennis slept.

The next morning, March 4, the day after Gerwing's last meeting with the Calverts, he took his Yukon in for service at an auto repair shop. He said he signed the necessary papers and then called for a taxi to take him to his offices at Sea Pines Center. A local taxi company verified that he was indeed a fare at 1:00 pm that afternoon—from the auto repair shop to The Club Group offices.

However, the cab company, and all other Hilton Head cab companies, verified in the investigation that they had no record of Gerwing calling for or being picked up at Sea Pines Center later that day or any other day surrounding the Calvert's disappearance. Gerwing had taken a cab to The Club Group, but left by some other means, leading investigators to believe that there might be a second party involved in Dennis's actions.

Chapter 10

Not An Ordinary Time

The 2008 swirl of Hilton Head activity was most unusual—resonating missing persons and mayhem. It was usually a tranquil island in winter and spring, awakening in summer with hustle and bustle as tourists crossed the bridge and headed for the grocery stores to stock up for the week of vacation that many had saved for all year.

Beginning each June, the parking lots were wild, as cars backed out of spaces at Publix and Harris Teeter—their drivers not looking, nearly missing other vehicles, and sometimes colliding with them. Mom and Dad and the kids pumped adrenalin—eager to get to that beach front home or golf course villa. Smiling motorists drove the highways, trying to see beyond trees and foliage that lined the main arteries, their necks trying to do a 180 to find restaurants and putt-putt courses that were, by local design, hidden from the road.

Thirty thousand souls expanded to more than 2 million during the summer months. Then, when the circus left town in the fall, quiet and order descended. The locals emerged from their gated communities and filled the tables in the finest restaurants on the island. "The 'terrorists' have gone," they would joke—and then say, "but we're sure glad they came."

The island that drew John and Elizabeth Calvert and Dennis Ger-wing would ordinarily return to a quiet serenity September through May. This time, however—this year—it was not to be. Foul things were afoot in February and March, and the island could kiss serenity goodbye.

It had happened before—Hilton Head and Daufuskie Islands had a rich history over several millennia, and peaceful times came and went. Native American Indians had once roamed these wide South Carolina beaches, only to be disrupted in 1663 when Captain William Hilton said goodbye to Northwich, Cheshire, England, crossed the Atlantic and sailed into Port Royal Sound, SC. He liked a particular island he saw and named what was to become one of America's favorite resorts—Hilton's Head.

The island, from the air, was unique. Captain Hilton was not privy to that perspective, but, had he been able to see it from 3,000 feet, he would have been surprised to see his namesake shaped like a shoe.

Located 30 miles from what is now Savannah, GA and 95 miles southwest of what is now Charleston, SC, the island stood out as a beautiful sight from the time man first saw it. Glistening white sand stretched for 12 miles along the Atlantic Ocean.

African slaves were once brought to Hilton Head to pick Sea Island Cotton—a much sought after commodity in European capitals where the crop became clothing for the wealthy. The Africans who picked the cotton would eventually become known as "Gullahs"—descen-dants of the Lowcountry South Carolina slaves who mixed Creole and African language in their speech.

The Sea Island Cotton industry the slaves bent to harvest would eventually fade—not so the Gullahs.

The Gullah tradition lived on throughout Hilton Head Island and extended across Calibogue Sound to Daufuskie—the southernmost occupied sea island in South Carolina. Daufuskie was five miles long and two and one-half miles wide. It was accessible only by boat and would remain isolated into the 21st century. On Daufuskie, a core of Gullah descendants lived on—a proud people who seemed to defy worldly wants and needs.

In the early 1700s, the southernmost tip of Daufuskie, "Bloody Point", earned its name as Yemassee natives stormed European settlements that had infiltrated the island. Spears and arrows were no match for modern weaponry, and the settlers massacred the Indians. Yemassee spirits were said to wander the island, crying out for their lost loved ones. At night, Daufuskie was a very spooky place to be.

Then, the Civil War and Hilton Head Island became the "Department of the South" for Union troops intent on blockading southern ports. Captain Hilton's island suddenly became a critical piece of land. In the aftermath, hundreds of escaped slaves descended upon Hilton Head shores. Many stayed, joining the Gullah population on both Hilton Head and Daufuskie.

For decades after the war the isolated barrier island of Hilton Head, on the Intracoastal Waterway, was sparsely inhabited until, one day, in the early 1950s a young Yale student by the name of Charles Fraser arrived. He was to spend the summer harvesting island trees from the tropical forest for his father's Georgia lumber business.

Fraser fell in love with the pristine island and convinced his father, General Joseph Bacon Fraser, to let him develop the real estate, rather than denude it. There followed, in the 50s, 60s and 70s, dramatic development that was protected environmentally by a set of covenants that Fraser created—covenants that were ultimately declared legal by the courts and that remain in effect today.

Fraser was insistent that his island become uniquely recognized. To achieve that, he built an iconic lighthouse, brilliantly striped in red and white colors. His lighthouse was called "Fraser's Folly"—but, just as Fraser had forecast, it became a beacon on the South Carolina coast—and Hilton Head became the model for high-end resorts along

America's southern seaboard.

The lure of his unique creation called mightily to lovers of sand and sea.

It was Karma—John and Elizabeth Calvert had no choice. They were inexorably drawn to the island named for Captain William Hilton and developed by Charles Elbert Fraser.

Chapter 11

★

Elizabeth Calvert

Elizabeth Calvert grew up in Atlanta, GA. She was a gregarious youngster at Fernbank Elementary School. By the time Liz reached high school at Druid Hills, the 5' 4" vivacious young woman had high goals in mind. She enrolled at Converse College in Spartanburg, SC after her high school years and there received her undergraduate degree. Even as a recent graduate, she was a booster for the school and would periodically host cocktail parties to raise money for the women's college.

Entering law school at the University of Georgia in 1987, Liz Calvert studied hard and graduated ready and poised for the legal world. It was not a glamorous start: the brown-haired blue-eyed graduate became a staff attorney at UPS in Atlanta. She worked hard for 14 years and climbed to the top of her sector—president of the legal department.

Elizabeth said goodbye to UPS when she received an offer from the prestigious Savannah law firm of Hunter Maclean. She joined the firm in 2007 to specialize in taxes, employee benefits, and executive compensation. She was aggressive, engaged in public service in

Savannah, and, slightly bored, sought new experiences.

Community organizations wanted her skill and intellect to support their causes. She was named to the board of the Georgia Conservancy and became a trustee at her alma mater. Her husband John enjoyed showering her with unusual gifts and one year presented her with a certificate for a flying lesson. She loved the experience of flying and decided to repeat it—many times. She earned her pilot's license in March 2006 and bought a plane, regularly winging out of Hilton Head Island airport in her Cirrus SR20—valued at $400,000.

She was alluring and adventurous, and an advertising supplement to *Forbes* Magazine featured Elizabeth Calvert, the winsome young pilot from Hilton Head Island. John Tatum, a partner at her law firm, was a fan. He told the *Island Packet*, "She was just first class, as a person, as a lawyer."

At UPS, she became a good friend with attorney Teri McClure. Seeking employment at UPS, Teri had interviewed with Elizabeth, who was then vice president of the legal department. Teri had no idea that, one day, she might become the last person with whom Liz Calvert would ever speak.

Over the years, Teri and Elizabeth lunched together, discussed jobs, politics, renovation of the Calvert's Atlanta home, and sundry matters. They remained close friends, even after Elizabeth left UPS. They spoke often by phone—they were close.

They were so close, in fact, that Teri was chatting on the phone with Elizabeth on March 3, 2008, as Elizabeth drove to that fateful meeting with Dennis Gerwing at Sea Pines Center. Teri told *Hilton Head Monthly* that Liz confided to her she had discovered problems with Calvert company financial records and she was on her way to confront her accountant, Dennis Gerwing.

Teri joked, "You better meet him in a public place." Teri said Liz laughed and responded that she expected no problems.

"She was the most trusting person. She did not conceive of anyone harming her. The fact that people do bad things was one of our on-going conversations. It just wasn't part of her nature," Teri said.

Elizabeth Calvert was 45 years old when she disappeared.

Chapter 12

★

John Calvert

John Calvert grew up in Greensboro, NC and received a degree in mechanical engineering at Georgia Tech in 1983. The handsome and prematurely grey Tech graduate proposed to Elizabeth while they were vacationing on Hilton Head Island—a place John dearly loved. They were married in 1998 and moved into a white brick home in Atlanta's historic Brookhaven district, just off Peachtree Road.

John worked many years for several power companies, including Duke Energy. In 2001, he took semi-retirement and then, in 2005, he ventured out on his own—inking the paper that made him the owner of four Hilton Head Island businesses. The Calverts then began to split their time between their Atlanta home and Harbour Town. John, a boating enthusiast, was in his element.

Friends described John as quiet and "not flashy", but he could be outgoing, according to his friend and Georgia Tech fraternity brother Mark Leinmiller. Elizabeth, on the other hand, Leinmiller said, had "a quick wit, but she's not going to be the life of the party. They balance each other."

John did have a whimsical side—he named his boat *Yellow Jacket*—celebrating the moniker of his Georgia Tech Yellow Jackets.

Leinmiller told the *Island Packet* that he had seen the Calverts shortly before they disappeared—at a friend's funeral in Atlanta. Leinmiller told Packet reporters, Tim Donnelly and Jim Faber, that it was entirely out of character for the couple to take off without notice, especially if it meant missing business obligations. "If you knew John and Liz, it just doesn't fit. It's like a 'Thelma and Louise' kind of thing, where they just disappear."

Lynn Johnston, who lived next door to the Calverts on Brookhaven Drive in the affluent Buckhead area of Atlanta, told *McClatchy Newspapers*, "John's a handyman around the house. He seemed to be very interested in making sure his businesses on the island succeeded."

Aside from the time John Calvert was on Hilton Head, reporters found there was a dearth of information about his background—graduate of Georgia Tech, fraternity boy, loved to sail, worked for Duke Energy—but that was about it.

"John Calvert? He was like a ghost. I was never able to pin down if John had any relatives," Dennis Gerwing's brother Fred said.

John was 47 years of age when he disappeared.

Chapter 13

★

Dennis Gerwing

Dennis Ray Gerwing had been on Hilton Head twenty years when his troubles began to magnify. He did not fit the persona of a killer or a cheat. It was hard to find any islander who did not like the cherubic Gerwing. Most who knew or encountered him said he was the quintessential "hail-fellow, well-met" guy.

Everyone remembered Dennis's laugh— "That great laugh," one friend said. Another Islander who loved Dennis Gerwing remembered him as having, "A smile and a glowing face."

Gerwing enjoyed life and the people in it. That smile his friends remembered lit up any room and folks looked forward to seeing him enter that room. Gerwing's obituary described him as, "A kind and generous person who helped many struggling people build better lives."

Dennis, his brother Fred, and sister Pat, grew up in Louisville, KY, children of a machinist, Morris, and Mary Helen, a schoolteacher.

Morris spoke to Mary Helen outside her church one day. He was on a Western Union bicycle, and he had a telegram for, "the girl in the green coat." The telegram asked Mary Helen to marry him. Mary Helen died of a brain aneurysm in 2006. Dennis's father, Morris, died of dementia following Dennis's death.

A hardworking young man with a broad grin, Dennis graduated from Bellarmine University in Louisville. While in college he married Dale Anderson from Louisville, who was studying to be a lawyer. The marriage lasted only one year, supposedly because they were separated—she remained in law school, and Dennis moved for employment purposes.

Nancy Barry, Dennis's first girlfriend after his marriage ended, believed that Dennis, who always called his mother Mary Helen, lost his moral compass when his mother died. Leaving Louisville was not difficult for Dennis, Nancy said—Dennis had found Louisville a town where it was difficult for him to enter "high society".

"Dennis liked 'old money,'" she said, "and he wanted to be accepted into that society."

So, he moved on.

After he achieved his goal of becoming a Certified Public Accountant, Arthur Andersen hired Dennis for their Indianapolis office. His work ethic quickly brought him to the attention of his superiors, and they offered him an opportunity to move up—to their offices in Denver.

The Denver office did accounting work for Ned Heizer at Resorts International, a company run by John Hemphill and John Platt. Hemphill and Platt subsequently hired Dennis as CFO of Vacation Resorts on Hilton Head. Dennis eagerly accepted the offer to move to the land of milk and honey. He had arrived in what he considered to be high society.

One year later, Vacation Resorts was sold to Ginn Holdings Corporation, and Dennis found himself working as head of finance and administration for them. Dennis rolled with the punches when real estate dominoes began to fall in the midst of a national recession, and the Ginn company was acquired by Luke M. Taylor, Jr. and Philip Schwab. He stayed on with the Taylor-Schwab Company, known as Hilton Head Holdings.

There, Dennis remained for a short while, but he would soon become a co-founder of The Club Group—a company built out of the ashes of Ginn Holdings Corporation.

Dennis Gerwing was 54 years old when he died.

Chapter 14

★

Honk If Bobby Owes You

Mark King and Dennis Gerwing met in the mid-1980s. It was a time when corporate holdings on Hilton Head Island were, to say the least, complicated. But, to understand the spider web of different ownership of Hilton Head developments, and the evolution of The Club Group, one needs to comprehend the chess moves that took place in the 1970s and 80s. It is not an easy task.

First, there was the mid-1970s oil crisis that slowed the influx to Hilton Head Island of over a million tourists each year. Second, there were the double-digit interest rates that loaded Sea Pines Company and its owner, Charles Fraser, with untenable debt demanded by lenders. Third, there was seemingly no way out but bankruptcy. Fraser lost all his holdings except Sea Pines Company.

Fraser was not alone—in 1971 iconic Hilton Head developer Fred Hack sold the Hilton Head Company to Philadelphia's Oxford First Corporation. Then, in 1980, Emro Land Company, a subsidiary of Marathon Oil, purchased the Hilton Head Company. Marathon redeveloped much of the Hilton Head Company's real estate holdings on the island and developed Wexford Plantation.

Sea Pines Company survived—for a while, but, in 1983, Fraser decided to sell his operating company and real estate to Vacation Resorts Inc., a subsidiary of venture group Heizer Corporation of Chicago. Vacation Resorts Inc. did not do well due to tax law changes and, as a result, Heizer decided to liquidate the Sea Pines assets in 1984.

The merry-go-round continued—it was difficult to keep up with the transactions. Before long, Marathon decided to sell its real estate holdings to an individual who would become a household name on Hilton Head Island—but not in a happy way. Thirty-six-year old E.R. "Bobby" Ginn III was a charismatic figure who had great enthusiasm and a creative mind.

Ginn had acquired Sea Pines in his buying binge and he fashioned a plan to create a holding company that would merge Marathon and Sea Pines assets. Bobby turned to the Savings and Loan Companies—an industry that would come on hard times as it struck deals that would later become fodder for federal investigations and legal proceedings.

The S&Ls loaned Ginn the money he needed, and when the smoke cleared, Bobby's roll-up saw him in control of Heizer Corporation's Vacation Resorts Inc. Properties (Sea Pines), and Marathon's considerable island holdings (Hilton Head Company).

Bobby lived the high life—a jet, a yacht—you name it. But, his kingdom would eventually come crashing down as ever-growing debt and internecine arguments roared through his corporation. Lawsuits grew precipitously, the PGA threatened to cancel the Heritage Golf Tournament unless Ginn could guarantee $650,000 in prize money, and bumper stickers appeared throughout the island that said, "Honk if Bobby Owes You!"

In 1986, multiple bankruptcies rocked the island like a roaring riptide. Charleston, SC Federal Judge Sol Blatt took charge. Blatt, who had never been engaged in a bankruptcy case, merged all the cases into one—it was, at that time, the largest bankruptcy case ever in the state of South Carolina.

Mark King was there to watch the tale unravel. He arrived on Hilton Head Island in 1972 and went to work for the original Hilton Head Company. King was there for 13 years and rose from golf professional to manager of the company's sports operations, including 5½ golf courses, two racquet clubs, and several professional golf and tennis tournaments.

Then, when Ginn merged the Sea Pines and Hilton Head sports operations under Ginn Holdings, King became senior vice president of all sports and tournament operations. He was in command of 10 ½ golf courses, 4 racquet clubs, 3 marinas, 5 tournaments (including the Family Circle Cup tennis tournament and The Heritage PGA tournament), and bicycle rentals—all his responsibility under Ginn Holdings.

Dennis Gerwing was senior vice president and chief financial officer for Ginn Holdings and worked there about a year and a half when it became evident Ginn was under-capitalized; several banks that had committed to provide refunding failed to come through.

In late 1986, Gerwing confided to Mark King, whom he had first met during company mergers in 1985, that the business for which they worked was on shaky ground. He went to Mark and said, "The future of Ginn Holdings is not good. You probably should be looking for something else."

So it was that in late 1986 and early 1987, Dennis and Mark decided to form The Club Group to manage golf courses. The young entrepreneurs were recognized as highly capable professionals, and as Ginn Holdings slid into bankruptcy, Marathon contacted The Club Group to work with them to help transition its Hilton Head Company assets out of bankruptcy, returning those assets to Marathon. The Club Group performed admirably, assisting David Axene, Marathon's appointed bankruptcy receiver. Marathon then hired The Club Group to manage its assets until they could be sold.

The Port Royal and Shipyard golf and tennis assets were sold to Avron Fogelman, a real estate developer and part-owner of the Kansas City Royals. Fogelman had purchased Harbour Town assets from bankruptcy proceedings and in late 1989, he hired The Club Group as consultants to help transition Harbour Town holdings to an entity that became known as Prudential-Bache/Fogelman Harbour Town Properties, L.P.

The Club Group also managed Port Royal and Shipyard Plantation golf and tennis properties; properties that Fogelman was trying to syndicate. Fogelman worked with Nations Bank in the endeavor, but the syndication was not a success and Nations Bank assumed control of the assets from Fogelman. The Club Group then assisted Nations Bank in selling Port Royal and Shipyard to The Beach Company of Charleston, SC.

Fogelman also asked The Club Group to manage the Harbour Town Properties. The Club Group agreed and did so, from 1998 until 2005—the year Prudential-Bache/Fogelman sold their lodging and marina businesses to John and Liz Calvert. The Calverts did not purchase the commercial and real estate properties.

King soon expanded The Club Group's reach to Savannah, GA, and Columbia, SC. The Club Group was on its way. Eventually, The Club Group would manage a number of courses in South Carolina and Georgia.

The Club Group had a growing brand—it was recognized as a good company to oversee resort properties and commercial operations. So it was that John and Elizabeth Calvert retained The Club Group to continue to provide administrative and accounting services for their lodging and marina businesses.

Then, issues arose.

"Liz wanted to get more involved in the business and that is where it came to light that she had accounting questions of Dennis regarding their accounts," Mark said.

"Later, it became known that she felt monies were missing from their accounts. Upon hearing this information, I immediately discussed this with Dennis and told him I felt the company needed to immediately engage an accounting firm to conduct a comprehensive forensic audit of all of our Hilton Head accounts. He agreed.

"After some research, I selected FTI, a world-renowned forensic accounting firm to conduct the audit. Within days we had engaged FTI and Dennis participated in a conference call with FTI where Dennis provided information on the accounting system the company used. FTI was scheduled to start the audit the next week.

"FTI, in a 30-day audit, discovered 8 out of 10 of our clients had missing funds, primarily from their reserve accounts, totaling $2.3 million. Chuck Scarminach and I formed a recovery committee that represented all eight of our affected clients and unveiled a plan as to how we were going to repay them.

"With help of two friends with MBAs, and attorney Scarminach, I was absolutely dedicated to repaying each and every dollar that was stolen. FTI's audit culminated the week of the Heritage Tournament," King said.

Mark King was a three-decade resident of Hilton Head Island and a highly regarded businessman whom clients and the public trusted implicitly. Their trust was rewarded.

"I immediately got with Fred Gerwing, Dennis's older brother, who wound up being the executor of Dennis's estate. Fred agreed to pledge all net proceeds from the estate to the recovery plan. I pledged, on behalf of The Club Group, to repay each and every one of the stolen dollars, using any and all monies we could find, and from profits from the company.

"I took out personal loans of $400,000 from two friends, which I loaned to The Club Group. That, along with several hundred thousand dollars that Fred was able to generate from the sale of Dennis's home in Hilton Head Plantation, was used to make an initial payment of $600,000 to our clients in May of 2008.

"Long story short, while it has taken 9 years, over $2.2 million, or approximately 97% of the money has now been repaid in its entirety, to those clients", King said. The company continues to make monthly payments and expects to achieve final repayment within two years.

"Monies were also missing from The Club Group, which we subordinated and never collected. My personal loans to the company were also subordinated and will never be repaid. I refinanced The Club Group debts to generate enough cash to repay the majority of the remaining debt to our clients," Mark said.

"I felt a very strong obligation to our existing Hilton Head clients. We had managed some of these properties for 20 years. Over this time, we had enjoyed excellent relationships both professional and personal. As an island resident for over 35 years it was very much a priority to make sure these folks were kept whole. Making full restitution was not the easiest thing to do, but I felt it was the right thing to do." King said.

Looking back, King said he thought he knew Dennis to be a kind, generous, and trusted business partner. Now, he's not sure at all that such was the case.

"Fred Gerwing and I tried to figure out where in the world Dennis could have gone off track. Fred seems to think it was when Dennis lost his mom—that he lost his moral compass at that point." Mark said.

Were Dennis, Liz and John compatible?

"Dennis and John were initially quite close. They went out to dinner quite a bit and became friends. When Liz got involved on the financial side of things, Dennis stated he had difficulty dealing with Liz,"

52

Mark said.

Where did all that money—millions—go?

"Early on, Fred Gerwing and I hoped we would find a large corpus of unspent money, but other than relative minor monies found in checking accounts and securities, there was nothing. It came to light that Dennis was doing quite a bit of day trading, some successful, some not. He had gotten into gambling, stuff he had never done from my and Fred's standpoint, prior to whatever happened to send him off in a different direction," Mark said.

"I'm not sure how well I knew him. He would have been the least likely person to embezzle money. He was quite anal to chase things to the penny if they did not balance. When it became evident that Dennis had embezzled money—this guy?" Mark said, shaking his head in disbelief.

"Then—he was named a person of interest—two people disappear— again, I question how well I knew him," Mark said, with obvious sadness that the person he considered a trusted business partner perhaps had a darker side.

"Investigators asked a number of our company employees here, 'Did you notice any dramatic change in Dennis?' The answer was, 'No not really, he was pretty much the same Dennis.' He probably traveled more than he did at one time, but other than buying a boat, there were no Rolex watches and that sort of thing," Mark said, thinking back.

"We were scheduled to start the audit the following week—the week he committed suicide," Mark said, with obvious heavy heart.

One person who knew Mark King marveled at King's pledge to pay back the debts he did not have to assume.

"He's a hell of a man," that person said, "Mark made a huge monetary sacrifice because he felt it was the right and only thing to do. It was very reminiscent of Mark's mentor Charles Fraser who, when forced to sell his holdings, bravely denied efforts to cut up his properties. It cost Fraser millions of dollars—but, it was the right thing to do."

Chapter 15

★

Nancy Barry

After moving to Hilton Head Island, Dennis Gerwing continued to maintain a stately brick home at 2401 Wilmot Avenue in Columbia, SC. It featured an elaborate kitchen and swimming pool and was located in a trendy Columbia neighborhood. The house was for sale for $1.2 million.

Dennis's girlfriend of 22 years, Nancy Barry, stayed in Columbia in Dennis's house. Dennis and Nancy had been estranged for about two years at the time of his death. She continued to speak of their relationship as, "Life Partners."

Nancy had met Dennis on Hilton Head Island when she was 24 and Dennis was 31. They first encountered each other on the *Compass Rose*, Charles Fraser's yacht. At the helm of the storied Fraser yacht was Captain Peter Ovens.

Captain Ovens, both hands on the wheel of the *Compass Rose*, saw the chemistry between Dennis and Nancy. The immaculate Fraser yacht splashed through waves and sailed majestically through Calibogue Sound as Ovens leaned toward Dennis and grinned broadly.

He pointed at Nancy and said to Dennis, "This is the girl for you."

And, indeed she was. Nancy described Dennis as, "Mr. Wonderful." She stayed on Hilton Head for two years before moving to her hometown of Columbia, SC—to live in Dennis Gerwing's house. Dennis, who fondly nicknamed Nancy his, "Big Girl", stayed on Hilton Head, but the romance continued. Later, he would christen his new boat the *Big Girl*, in honor of Nancy.

"Dennis was a good man and always did the right thing. He supported me working and having my own life. I worked for an orthopedic surgeon for 13 years and a neurosurgeon for 17 years," Nancy said in a statement to the Sheriff's Office and obtained in the FOIA.

Dennis bought Nancy a car and, one day, the car disappeared. Nancy filed a police report. The car had been repossessed for non-payment. Dennis paid off the car debt, and he took care of all the house bills, even though he and Nancy were separated.

"Dennis was not a slacker," Nancy said. "He would come up every weekend during the twenty years we were together. He would clean the gutters at the house, and he worked with the yard crews when they were there. He was physically involved in taking care of the house. His landscape director, Walter, was very sad when Dennis died," Nancy said.

She added, "Dennis was brilliant, chauvinistic, and thoroughly enthralled by (Sea Pines founder) Charles E. Fraser."

She told a friend that Dennis never used drugs. "He was 100 percent anti-drug. He loved his red wine," Nancy said.

Nancy told SLED Special Agents Kevin Baker and Freddie Pough that she had received a call from Dennis on March 6, 2008 between 7:30 am and 8:30 am. Gerwing had advised her he was going to the Beaufort County Sheriff's Office to talk with them about the Calverts. Gerwing told her that he had a business meeting with the Calverts on Monday, March 3, at his office around 6:00 pm. He told her after he left the meeting he went home, cooked dinner, ate, and returned to work.

"Why do the police want to talk with you?" she asked.

"They probably want to speak with me because I was the last person to see the Calverts alive," Dennis answered.

Barry said she again spoke by phone with Dennis on Saturday, March 8. Gerwing told her he was staying on Hilton Head because the police were serving a search warrant on his residence and car. He would stay that night, he said, with his friend Forest "Dan" Duryea, at his home. It would be Dan Duryea who would later call Nancy's Columbia friend Ann Bellamy to ask her to inform Nancy that Dennis was dead.

Nancy last heard from Dennis on Monday, March 10. It was around 4:30 pm and Dennis said he was calling from his attorney's office. He said he would not be coming to Columbia because "things weren't looking good." He told Nancy he was a "person of interest" and that he might be the last person to see the Calverts alive.

Nancy later said, "Dan Duryea and his wife Tammy were probably Dennis's only real friends. Dan helped Dennis and The Club Group develop Timberlake in Columbia (developed by Mark King, Mike McKee, and Dennis). Dennis spent the last few nights of his life with Dan."

Barry said Dennis never discussed business or money matters with her. She stated that they did, together, have a "household" bank account at NBSC that Gerwing would put money into for her to write checks for household expenses. "He would put anywhere from $1,000 to $1,500 at a time into the account," she said.

Nancy did recount later that Dennis had a will and she was the beneficiary. But, she said, when Dennis wrote his suicide note, he left everything to Mark King. Nancy confirmed that she was "so out of it" that she, as the named executor, permitted Dennis's brother Fred Gerwing to execute the will. Then she said she thought Mark King might have executed the will, she was not sure.

"Was Dennis ever in a physical altercation with you in your 20 years of relationship?" Special Agent Baker asked.

"No," she said, adding that Gerwing had raised his voice to her on occasion when they would argue, but he never physically harmed her. Barry stated that Dennis was a gentleman.

"Did he gamble?" the agent asked.

"I do not know of his gambling," she said. However, she stated that they had been estranged for about two years. She was not aware of Dennis dating any other woman.

But, there *were* other women.

Chapter 16

★

Laura Merrill

D ennis had found a new girlfriend on Hilton Head Island. On March 11, 2008, Detective Bob Bromage, with Michael Prodan and Carl Sesly, interviewed Laura Merrill at the Hilton Head office of the BCSO. During the interview, Bromage's report said, her husband was present. The following is from Bromage's report:

Laura Merrill…who was identified as a close friend and companion of Gerwing was interviewed at the Hilton Head BCSO Office on 03-11-2008 at 7:30 pm. Present during the interview were Michael Prodan (SLED/BSU) and Carl Sesley (RCMP/BAU). During the majority of the interview, Laura Merrill was accompanied by her husband (Robert Merrill)…The interview was taped surreptitiously by use of a Sony Digital Recorder.

Laura Merrill advised that she met Gerwing a few years ago through her employment and fellow associates at the Diamond Club. She advised that Gerwing made an arrangement with her and her husband that he would pay for her to spend time with him. She advised that they went on trips together and Gerwing would pay her for her time and being away from her family.

She advised that she was one of his closest friends and spoke with him or sent text messages back and forth with him almost every day. Gerwing's mobile telephone number was identified as 843-290-2491.

When asked specifically about 03-03-2008 and any contact that she had with Gerwing, she advised that he had sent a text to her at 7:39 pm. She pulled up the text on her telephone and it read "Hi sorry I missed ur call. Met w-my buddies tonight and they didn't even invite me to dinner. I'm heading home".

She showed us where she sent a text message back to him at 9:02 pm to let him know that she was trying to call him and advised that she did not hear back from him until the next day.

At 1:21 pm on 03-04-2008, she sent him a text "Hello R u alive?" and he responded at 1:22 pm, stating, "Hi...Yes still breathing. It's been very hectic." There were several small talk text messages back and forth after that point. Merrill advised that she was aware that he was being accused of embezzling $200,000 by the Calverts in conversations she had with Gerwing.

She stated that she did not see Gerwing on 03-03-2008 and has no knowledge of the whereabouts of the Calverts.

She advised that she is a student at Savannah College of Art and Design and was at school late on 03-03-2008, arriving home at approximately 9:30 pm. Further stating that she did not leave again that night. Robert Merrill advised that he arrived home from work between 5:30 pm and 6 pm and did not leave again on 03-03-2008.

It was not until October, 2008 that Robert Merrill received a polygraph test regarding his statements. Detective Bromage said Laura Merrill was not polygraphed. Here is his report of Robert Merrill's polygraph:

On 10-30-2008, a polygraph examination was administered to Robert Merrill by Msgt Averill at the BCSO Law Enforcement Center regarding his knowledge of the disappearance of the Calverts. He was identified as being associated with Dennis Gerwing in business and friendship.

Msgt Averill reported that Merrill was truthful during the polygraph examination.

I contacted Lt. Michael Wilkins of the Savannah/Chatham Metro Police Department for his assistance in establishing Laura Merrill's alibi for March 3, 2008, as she advised that she was in class at the Savannah College of Art and Design until evening hours. It was established that her student identification was utilized to enter the college at 4:55 pm on that date. As of this time, it would appear based on this information that she was truthful about her whereabouts.

On October 23, 2008, polygraph examiner Matthew Averill submitted an "Investigative Polygraph Report" that said there was no deception in Robert Merrill's polygraph test. He listed the "relevant questions" as:

(R5) Did you participate in the disappearance of the Calvert's? Answer: No

(R7) Did you assist anyone in causing the disappearance of the Calvert's? Answer: No

(R10) Do you know the location of the Calvert's? Answer: No

Chapter 17

The Calibogue Cay Years

Dennis Gerwing prospered in his work on Hilton Head and purchased a home in one of the toniest areas of the resort paradise. The narrow strip at the south end of the island where he bought was called "Calibogue Cay"—uber-expensive real estate with multi-million dollar homes that featured state-of-the-art docking facilities for their fishing boats and high-end yachts.

Dennis liked the location. His brother Fred said Dennis used the house as a rental property. He lived in another house with Dan Duryea two doors down. The house in which he lived faced deep water. His visitors made a right-hand turn onto the street and found the house three doors down, on the left. It featured a magnificent sunset view over Calibogue Sound. Oddly enough, Fred said, the elite home had just two bedrooms.

Occasionally, Dennis would wave at passing boats from his waterside backyard and invite those aboard to pull up to his dock and join one of his lovely parties. "That was just Dennis, a great guy," one partier who accepted a number of the seagoing invitations said.

Down by the docks at Harbour Town, Peter Ovens, who knew Dennis well, said, "When I took him sailing he would take out eight or ten friends. He always invited my crew and me to dinner afterward—we were included in the party."

"He was nice and never seemed scary. He just got himself pushed into a corner where he could not get out. Good people do bad things," a long-time island resident who knew Dennis well said, her voice trailing off with palpable sadness.

Club Group executive Bob Long was also saddened by the turn of events for Dennis Gerwing, "I loved Dennis," Long said, "he was a true renaissance man, just a lovely person. He was a great cook and gave wonderful parties. I just have a hard time believing it."

Chapter 18

Strippers & A Gambling Habit

One day, Dennis Gerwing, fascinated by different people, called storied Hilton Head Boat Captain Peter Ovens and said he had a group he wanted to take out on Peter's classic boat, the *Schooner Welcome*. Peter said, "Dennis arrived boat side with five strippers from the local strip club. I kept a straight face and invited the ladies aboard and set sail. It was fun. Dennis was a great host, and nothing happened. The ladies were Girl Scouts," Captain Ovens said.

Dennis later sold the waterfront home he owned on Calibogue Cay and moved to Hilton Head Plantation and into a $430,000 residence on the north end of the island. In his home, he placed a myriad of pictures taken with buddies on trips to the Arctic Circle, Patagonia, the Sahara, and other distant locales. Dennis was an exceptional photographer, and many of his photos were in the pages of *National Geographic* Magazine.

Arthur Suggs, a friend from former employment, wrote fondly in a funereal remembrance of one of those travels with Dennis:

"Dennis, you were my 'boss man' and my friend, and you will be missed by me on both levels. We still have some more traveling to do and photographs to take. My condolences and best wishes to your family and friends. I miss you, my friend."

Dennis's brother Fred said, "He pretty much stayed on the go all the time. He was a great guy and generous. He wouldn't hurt a fly."

Dennis's countenance was such that friends described him as a "mild-mannered wine connoisseur." "He handled a lot of money for people," Beaufort County Sheriff's Office Detective Bob Bromage said.

Everything seemed mostly positive about Dennis Gerwing—but, the laughing, affable, fun-loving and mild-mannered accountant was reported to have a gambling habit, and rumors said that he was heavily in debt. No one mentioned where his suspected betting pattern took place.

On Sunday, February 24, 2008, Dennis said in an email to his new lady friend Laura:

"I received in the mail, an invitation to Harrah's New Orleans. The charter plane leaves Jacksonville on fri apr 18 and returns on sun apr 20. I think that is the golf tournament weekend. If I promise to curtail my "addiction" (...unless, of course, I'm winning and then I know u wouldn't let me) would u like to go to New Orleans for a weekend?...and yes this is in addition to the long weekend in Cancun. Let me know so I can book it. Hope u r having a good day...mine has been great. It started w/a 1 ½ hr bike ride this morning. Xxxxxxooo"

Several casino receipts were discovered in Dennis's residence. His family knew that he took frequent trips to casinos around the United States. In May 2000, records showed, Dennis had played the tables at the Majestic Star Casino in Indiana.

Nancy Barry said, "There were many books on gambling at Dennis's residence at 8 Bent Tree Road. Dennis gambled on a trip to St. Louis where he had meant to visit his father."

Dennis loved the games at home, as well. Rumor had it that he spent a lot of time at a local "casino"—a home in Wexford Plantation that was the site of gambling fun and games. Rumors said Dennis was a high roller at the card tables there, spending lots of money.

The rumors became magnified, and it was mentioned that Dennis regularly flew to Russia to gamble. Island tales flew wildly and cocktail hour conversation along Harbour Town Golf Links feasted on speculation that Russian prostitutes were regulars at the Wexford gambling house where men played poker and—who knew what else was going on?

The manager of an island strip club identified Gerwing as a frequent customer, and there was gossip Dennis hired "escorts." On top of all that, Gerwing had used his finances, or those of others, to back a restaurant in Savannah, and he supposedly had lost heavily in the stock market.

A call to the Sheriff's Office was received—it was a woman that had worked with Dennis at The Club Group. She said that she knew Dennis frequented the "Gentleman's Club" on the island and acted as if he were a celebrity when he was there. The officer who received the call quoted her as saying, "He had one particular girl that was 'his'."

Dennis Gerwing's brother Fred said, "I know Dennis and John Calvert went to strip clubs together. There is no question in my mind that John was a heavy drinker. I saw him inebriated on many occasions. He was just a mess."

Fred added, "I did not see John and Elizabeth as a loving couple—it was a business partnership. I told Dennis when he said he was going to get in business with the Calverts that he should be careful. I told him I did not trust them."

Most people knew Dennis and John to be very close friends.

Chapter 19

★

From Russia—With Love?

Then a new twist—a Russian woman who danced at The Diamond Club on Hilton Head. The dancer, Anya Bateava, got into trouble at the club and Dennis agreed to help her. One of the other dancers had turned her into Immigration because she was illegally in the country. A friend said she had apparently married on Hilton Head to develop residency, but when her husband was questioned about her, he denied everything, leaving Anya without complete documentation.

A July 27, 2008 Beaufort County Sheriff's supplemental incident report by Sergeant Angela Viens said:

I called Anna Bateava (several words here were redacted) on 03-21-08, who said that she was now residing in Krasodr [sic], Russia. Bateava identified Dennis Gerwing as her "friend". She said that they met three years ago through Laura Merrill, when she was working at Kuramas restaurant. She said that she did not know of Dennis Gerwing prior to moving to Hilton Head. She said that she met and married a man named John Rubinsak who operates S and J Taxi service. She said that she spoke to Gerwing approximately three weeks prior to my call to her and usually speaks to him about twice a month. She said that she was deported by Immigration after *her husband failed to follow through in helping her with citizenship papers. She initially came to the United States on a student visa and overstayed to work and save money. She said that she gave Dennis Gerwing $5,000.00 to invest for her. She learned of Dennis Gerwing's suicide through Laura Merrill. Bateava stated that she did not talk to Gerwing about the Calvert's disappearance.*

Immigration officials arrested Anya, and Dennis retained an attorney for her. The government moved her to Charleston, SC, by one account, and to Alabama, by another account, to await deportation. Dennis then traveled to her location to keep her company. Upon deportation, she located in Budapest and Dennis flew there to be with her.

In Budapest, he arranged for Anya to obtain schooling. He kept friends on Hilton Head updated on her whereabouts and activities, and they could tell he was very proud of how well she was doing—"tops in her class."

On Hilton Head, over sushi one evening, Gerwing told his friend Lesly Crick that Laura Merrill was acting a little jealous of his relationship with Anya.

"I didn't really know much about his relationship with her, but I did know that he traveled to Paris with her. While he was there, he got his wallet stolen, so I wired him some money, which he paid back when he returned," Lesly said.

On March 26, Sergeant Viens and Master Sergeant Michael Riley met with Anya's former husband, John Rubinsak.

"I met her two years ago when she rented a room from me," he told Viens. He said she worked at the Diamond Club.
"We got to be very good friends and had a personal relationship," Rubinsak told Viens. He and Anya married on September 22, 2006. Then, in October of 2006, she was gone—they had lived together for one year. He said they slept in separate rooms, even after they

70

were married.

The husband told Viens he received a call from his wife on what he remembered to be October 10. He said she told him two men from Immigration came and took her away. They moved her to Charleston, SC, he said, and she was deported from that port. He said he had not heard from her since.

"Did you get married in an effort for her to gain citizenship?" Viens asked.

The husband said no, "We got married because we were more than roommates." Under further questioning, he denied that anyone ever paid him to marry Anya or asked him to marry her.

Viens asked if Anya had left a large sum of money behind that was collected from his residence by Dennis Gerwing or an associate of his, and the husband denied any such allegation. He said he did not know Dennis Gerwing and had never heard of him.

"Her stuff was cleaned out by a few Mexican girls, and a local man came and picked up the stuff." He said he was not aware of anyone managing his wife's money.

Fred Gerwing had a different story. He said Anya was, "part of a mail-order bride gig." Fred said she told Dennis she had a suitcase under her bed with, "$20,000 in cash in it." Fred said he assumed it was money she had saved from her "business".

Dennis, Fred said, went to Anya's house to retrieve her belongings. But, the husband, Dennis told Fred, was very uncooperative.

"Dennis said, "The guy was a total jerk, and the house was nasty," Fred said.

Fred continued, saying, "Dennis took Rob Merrill with him as a 'strong arm', and Rob pinned Anya's husband to the wall while Dennis reached under her bed and took the suitcase with the money."

"Later," Fred said, "Dennis took the money and deposited it in a Wachovia Bank account and moved it to Anya for her education. I have a deposit ticket on Wachovia Bank on March 6 of 2007 for $20,000."

Anya supposedly had not been alone on Hilton Head—she was said to have had Russian friends at Ocean Walk Villas who worked with her at The Diamond Club.

Chapter 20

Chuck Scarminach & Dan Saxon

The law firm of Novit & Scarminach represented The Club Group. Chuck Scarminach was the legendary Hilton Head lawyer who knew everyone on the island. The Syracuse, New York barrister was proud of his Italian descent and was a swashbuckling presence that captivated anyone who came within his broad spectrum of influence.

One could sit and listen to Chuck Scarminach stories for hours. A raconteur supreme, Scarminach, behind those bushy eyebrows, wide smile and sparkling eyes, possessed a keen intellect and instincts that made him a stellar attorney.

Practicing with Scarminach was a lawyer by the name of Dan Saxon. Saxon, a Lowcountry native, practiced business and property law and occasionally entered the courtroom as a litigator. He and Scarminach held one another in high regard and loved to engage in badinage. They were very, very good at what they did. The Club Group had chosen well its legal counsel, and Dennis Gerwing benefitted from its choice.

Scarminach had worked with Dennis during Gerwing's employment as a financial officer of the Sea Pines Company, a client of his firm. Later, when Mark King and Dennis formed The Club Group, Ltd.,they retained Novit & Scarminach as counsel for the business. Dennis then came to rely on Chuck Scarminach's advice in personal matters—the case for many executives of Scarminach's corporate clients.

The first awareness Scarminach had that his Club Group work in March 2008 would be a bit different than usual occurred one day with a call from The Club Group CEO Mark King.

"Mark said, 'We need your assistance'," Scarminach recalled.

"I'm thinking it's something financial," Scarminach said.

He went on.

Mark says, "The Calverts are missing. We are going to be questioned."

"All of it, initially, was low key," Scarminach said, but he was shocked that Dennis Gerwing was even considered as connected to the disappearance of the Calverts.

"Dennis Gerwing?" Scarminach said, "He was a nebbish!"

"Nebbish"—the word is defined as—"timid, or weak", but Scarminach had held Dennis in high esteem and never would have considered him to be a person who would be suspected of wrongdoing.

When Dennis was finally said to be a possible person of interest in the Calvert case, Scarminach's first comment was, "Are you kidding me?"

Late in the day on March 5, the telephone rang in Gerwing's office. It was the Beaufort County Sheriff's Office. "Would Dennis come in for a follow-up interview and polygraph the next day, March 6?"

"Am I a suspect?" Dennis asked.

The response was "No"—the Sheriff's Office just needed to chat with Dennis once again.

Reluctantly, Gerwing agreed to go to the Sheriff's office the next day, as requested. He hung up the phone. But, he thought about it. A lot. What was the right thing to do? What was the right thing for Dennis Gerwing?

The next morning, before going to the Sheriff's Office, Gerwing visited the offices of Novit & Scarminach. There, he told Dan Saxon he was due at the Sheriff's Office in 20 minutes—to undergo yet another round of interrogation.

Saxon knew Gerwing had been interrogated for five hours on the first investigative go-round. Scarminach was also aware that Dennis had cooperated with the Sheriff's Office in every way he could. The veteran attorney shook his head in disbelief and said, "Anything they've asked for, if they asked for it, he's given it to them."

"Dennis, you might not want to do that," Saxon said, addressing the request that Dennis again undergo interrogation. Saxon added, "Let me tell the Sheriff's Office you're not going to make a statement until we talk."

Dennis agreed with the advice regarding the requested second interrogation and Saxon went, by himself, to the Sheriff's Office. There, Saxon told the officer with whom Dennis was to meet that Gerwing was his client.

"Based on my conversation with the deputy, it was pretty clear to me they considered Dennis more than just a witness," Saxon said. "I think he (the deputy) was very unhappy because a lawyer was now involved and he knew Dennis would not likely be making any further statements," Saxon said.

The deputy was correct—Saxon said Dennis would not speak with the Sheriff's Office again—any further questions were to be addressed to his attorney.

"My recollection is that the conversation ended with the deputy's comment of, 'I would think Mr. Gerwing would want to come down immediately and cooperate to clear his name.' It was after that conversation that I advised Dennis to speak with and retain a criminal attorney," Saxon said.

Gerwing took Saxon's advice to retain criminal counsel and made contact with Cory Fleming, a well-known South Carolina criminal lawyer with the law firm of Moss, Kuhn & Fleming in Beaufort County. Fleming immediately agreed Gerwing should not keep the Sheriff's appointment and that he should have no further contact with the Sheriff's office.

"We never talked with him (Gerwing) again," Detective Bob Bromage said.

Chapter 21

★

Going To The Dogs

On March 6, the Behavioral Science Unit of the South Carolina Law Enforcement Division (SLED) entered the Calvert case as cable news channels parked their satellite trucks near the entrance of Sea Pines. Two criminal profilers agreed to assist with investigative strategies. The Federal Bureau of Investigation (FBI) also offered its services. Additionally, the Hilton Head Island Fire and Rescue Division agreed to provide personnel to assist in the search.

"We've gotten a lot of calls from all over the country," said Captain Toby McSwain, head of the Beaufort County Sheriff's Office southern division. "It's been a while since I remember seeing this many calls."

At about the same time, K-9 Unit personnel began ground searches of the areas that might have provided easy access to dispose of the Calvert's bodies. Dogs and investigators searched vast regions square foot by square foot, including most of Sea Pines and the Sea Pines Forest Preserve. They also combed the wooded area behind Sea Pines Center and donned gloves to fish through hundreds of trash containers. They found nothing of interest.

As the search went on, business associates of the Calverts and Gerwing were interviewed—extensively. Multiple areas on and around Hilton Head Island, as well as areas off-island, were searched—exhaustively. An FBI aviation unit conducted an aerial search of the island and its waterways, to no avail. SLED and the US Coast Guard followed with an air unit search and also came up empty.

Dive units penetrated island lagoons, waterways and Harbour Town Marina, finding nothing. An intensive door-to-door search of every rental villa managed by The Club Group was conducted.

Bubba Gillis, the owner of Cardinal Court Storage, was in his office when Sheriff's deputies entered the business, advising Gillis his storage bays would be searched. Gillis said he was told they were searching every storage facility on Hilton Head.

Throughout that day, and for days to follow, storage facility bays on the island were opened and thoroughly probed. Nothing of interest to the case was found. A Royal Canadian Mounted Police officer on loan from the RCMP, who was a behavioral science specialist in geographic profiling, pinpointed areas that should be searched. Sheriff's deputies and SLED police combed the sectors the RCMP officer highlighted and found no trace of bodies or body parts.

Chapter 22

John Calvert's Mercedes-Benz Is Found

On March 7, the silver Mercedes John Calvert owned was found at around 3:00 am in the parking lot of the Hilton Head Marriott Resort & Spa in Palmetto Dunes off Hwy. 278.

"It's an E320 Mercedes with a Georgia Tech tag, GT821B," came the report from Sheriff's Office Lieutenant Corporal Jon Klein, who wrote, "The vehicle was covered in pollen along with other small leaves and sticks. In an attempt to locate additional physical evidence, I searched the area of the parking lot where the vehicle was parked but was met with negative contact."

The Mercedes had last been seen parked six miles away at Sea Pines Center on March 3, the night of the last Calvert meeting with Dennis Gerwing. State Police were alerted, and a SLED Crime Scene Unit was soon scouring and securing the hotel parking lot. They then turned to the luxury automobile.

Experts went over the car in minute detail and found it to be pristine, except for empty coffee cups on the front passenger seat, an indication that just one person was in the car when it entered its parking space. SLED checked for biological and latent evidence in, on, or around the car.

SLED then towed the car to the Hilton Head Island Fire and Rescue station in Palmetto Dunes to shelter the vehicle, further collecting and analyzing its contents to capture any scintilla of information relating to the Calvert disappearances.

Detective Bob Bromage walked through the door of the Fire Station and began to circle John Calvert's vehicle. He focused in on the exterior of the driver's side rear door where he was suspicious of two stains.

"Swab it," he said, ordering further investigation. Both stains were then swabbed to obtain a sample of the source of the stains for future laboratory analysis. The swabs were submitted to the Sheriff's Office Evidence Repository. The Sheriff's Office, relentless, was leaving no stone unturned.

However, all efforts to find clues of value in, on, or around the 2006 Mercedes proved fruitless. The forensic process was applied to Elizabeth Calvert's Mini Cooper, with the same result.

What about video surveillance of the hotel parking lot?

Well, yes, there was such surveillance, but, as reported by ABC News, it was unclear if the surveillance video trained on the lot captured Calvert, or anyone else, leaving the car at the hotel.

Even though the abandoned car gave no clue as to John Calvert's whereabouts, islander Tony Gibbus did not fret for Calvert's safety, saying, "John Calvert makes his own luck. If you had to get out of a sticky situation, he'd be the guy you want with you."

Island Packet reporters Daniel Brownstein and Tim Donnelly covered in full detail the "Calvert Car Found!" story. The *Packet*, above the fold and on the front page, presented the new material. Was it a breakthrough?

Well, at least John Calvert's Mercedes was now another piece of the puzzle to place on the table as Brownstein and Donnelly tried to fit together the baffling questions that remained.

They were not alone in trying to solve that puzzle. The Beaufort County Sheriff's Office, SLED, the FBI, cadaver dogs, divers, forensic experts, shrimpers, fishermen, kids on bicycles, and area housewives were also on the alert and in on the search.

Slowly, a slight fear began to creep into islanders' minds as they contemplated the disappearance of two prominent and well-liked business people. Was there a predator on the island? Should ordinary folk be concerned for their well-being?

Online postings gave credence to the fear factor. One said, "Lately, it seems like open season on people whereas they end up missing and the cars are found. I don't mean to sound paranoid, but I'm getting to where I don't like to drive at night by myself or drive long trips by myself."

One response to the posting said, "Honey, I totally know what you're saying! I left the grocery yesterday and called hubby on the phone to say I be [sic] home shortly…a less than 10-mile drive. I have my key ready before I leave a store, look around to see who's around my car and thankfully, my car doors lock automatically when I start the engine. You just can't be too safe anymore."

Chapter 23

Red Fish & A Tear In The Eye

Dennis Gerwing spent a stressful day on March 7, 2008. He was a regular at the Red Fish Restaurant on Palmetto Bay Road and entered the restaurant that night for dinner and some relaxation.

Pleasantries were exchanged with a smiling greeter as Dennis walked through the door, passing the racks of wine and white tablecloths that topped the many tables in one of the island's very favorite eating venues. Red Fish employees shared their hellos as Dennis walked through the establishment, greeting the affable Gerwing—he was a fellow they were always glad to see.

"How are you doing, Dennis?" one staffer said with a smile, pouring a Pinot Noir that Gerwing, known for his wine acumen, had ordered.

"A tear came into Dennis's eye when asked how he was doing," the waiter remembered.

Dennis said, "It's been a rough week. The cops think I did it."

"What?"

"The Sheriff's Office has been tailing me, and they've searched my house and cars," Dennis said.

Red Fish employees stopped in their tracks. They did not believe Gerwing was involved in anything questionable.

"I've known him for years," one said, "he'd give you the shirt off his back. Dennis has helped a lot of people."

Red Fish owner Rick Peterson knew Dennis and John Calvert from their frequent visits to the restaurant. "They drank Pinot Noir," Peterson said.

Peterson recalled arriving home from vacation in early March of 2008. "It was the night before Dennis passed away. I was with Chuck Loeb (the award-winning guitarist who played with Stan Getz) and our wives. We walked into Red Fish, and there was Dennis. He was alone at the bar."

Peterson walked over to Dennis and put his hand on his shoulder.

"Hey, Dennis, I am so sorry to hear about your friends," Peterson said, referencing the Calverts.

"Horrible!" Dennis said, turning to Peterson, a fearful look in his eye. He then added, "I am frightened."

"Why?" Peterson asked, concerned.

"The police are following me," Dennis said, shaking his head in disbelief. "They think I might be involved."

"That's ridiculous!" Peterson said.

"John and I did a deal together, and Elizabeth found out about it and got angry," Dennis said.

"That's horrible," Peterson said. He could not help noticing scratches on Dennis's hand.

"How did you hurt your hand?" Peterson asked, pointing to the web of Gerwing's right hand.

"Gardening," Dennis replied.

"Then, Dennis started to cry, and I tried to console him," Peterson recalled.

"Dennis, if you need a place to stay, you can stay in our guest room," Peterson said, again placing his hand on Dennis's shoulder.

"I appreciate it," Dennis said, looking up at Peterson with gratitude.

"Dennis was an anomaly, from my perspective he was a lovely guy," Peterson said, obviously saddened by Dennis's death.

"I Googled the death style and found the method used was a favorite of the Russian mob. Stabbing—there," Peterson said, referencing Dennis's wound to his inner thigh.

Peterson had also met Dennis's lady friend, Laura Merrill, the Russian dancer.

"Dennis had a girl at a topless place, and he brought her family over here," Peterson said, referencing his restaurant.

"They came to Red Fish for dinner one night, and I met her and her brother and two sisters," Peterson recalled.

"Dennis said he would be doing business with the girl's father, buying used tractors and other equipment, shipping them to Kazakhstan (formerly in the USSR) where they would be sold," Peterson said.

Chapter 24

"Things Aren't Looking Good"

Dennis's brother Fred Gerwing knew his brother well—and he knew Dennis was not always quiet and affable.

"Most of the time Dennis was a happy-go-lucky guy. But—he did have a temper. He was not, however, vindictive. He would rather play a chess game with these guys. He would not let Liz (Calvert) catch him short on some accounts. He got caught in a time frame where he could not cover the money he took.

"When Liz decided to leave Atlanta, and come back and stick her nose in the business, it was a mess. Dennis said he had to get Liz and John together so John would own up as to what was going on," Fred said.

The investigation moved forward, and on March 5, within a few hours of questioning Dennis Gerwing, Sheriff's Office investigators considered him a person of interest in the disappearance of John and Elizabeth Calvert—they would not so name him until March 11.

Dennis was worried, no doubt. He telephoned Nancy Barry in Columbia, and told her he was going to talk to the Beaufort County

Sheriff's Office Investigators because he "was the last person to see them alive."

He said the same thing to *People Magazine*, "It's possible I was the last person who saw them." He then became wary and refused to comment further to *People* about the business meetings or anything else connected with the case. *People* then turned to Mark King as The Club Group CEO, and King told the magazine his company was "actively cooperating with police, who have asked us not to comment."

But, Dennis Gerwing did not stop talking about the case with Nancy Barry, saying, "Things aren't looking good," and that he was "a person of interest."

Chapter 25

★

"Do It Again!"

On March 8 Gerwing agreed to have his home, business office and vehicles searched. The Sheriff's Office obtained search warrants and began to look for biological and latent evidence of any foul play.

Gerwing alerted attorney Dan Saxon who went to Dennis's home at 8 Bent Tree Lane in Hilton Head Plantation to monitor the search with Dennis.

Investigators were hard at work. They found a small pile of dirt in the kitchen area, something they said was not characteristic of Dennis's otherwise tidy house. Dennis said the dirt came from a pair of white running shoes nestled beside the dirt.

A shovel with dirt on the bottom was found near the side door of the home—Dennis explained that he had been repairing his irrigation system—a sprinkler in the front yard had malfunctioned.

"Let's take a look," the investigator said.

They walked to the front yard. There was no evidence of fresh digging anywhere in the yard.

"I was not successful in fixing it," Dennis explained.

Dennis said there was a broken wine bottle in the kitchen. Gerwing said he had dropped it. Investigators asked Gerwing to show them where he had broken the bottle. He did so. There was no evidence of blood or broken glass at that location.

Officers noted in their inspection report, "The cuts on his hand did not appear to be consistent with a cut from a wine bottle."

Oddly enough, Dennis's garage contained many washers and dryers—probably appliances that had been replaced in properties The Club Group managed.

All trash containers in and outside Gerwing's residence were carefully examined. Investigators searched for the broken wine bottle Gerwing said had been the cause of the laceration on his right hand. There was trash from many days prior, but no broken wine bottle was found.

Then, both vehicles Gerwing owned were searched for blood evidence. A section of rope was found in the trunk of Dennis's Toyota Avalon, but no conclusions were drawn.

Forensic experts from SLED moved on to Dennis's GMC Yukon and found that the third-row seat had been removed. Gerwing said he had removed the seat to move furniture. Investigative reports found that Dennis's claim was never substantiated in interviews with his work associates and close friends.

The search of the Yukon was performed in great detail. Two SLED officers sprayed Luminol (a chemical that exhibits chemiluminescence with a blue glow to detect trace amounts of blood at a crime scene) throughout the vehicle—which left a white-to-pale yellow crystalline solid that covered the interior of the Yukon vehicle.

Saxon said, "They finished their inspection late in the evening and said, "Nothing here.""

The Sheriff's Office said, "Do it again!" Saxon recalled.

One of the SLED officers replied, "No, not doing it again, nothing here!" Saxon said. The officers, two women, were driving back to Columbia that evening and, at 10:00 at night, were in no mood to do the search again. Saxon said they refused the request.

Why did the Sheriff's Office insist— "Do it again?

Well, some assumed the Sheriff's Office had determined that Gerwing was the culprit in the Calvert disappearance and detectives were pushing hard to prove that— "Do it again!"

Investigative search of Dennis's home was noted in an official report: *Several items were seized from the residence including a computer (Compaq CPU serial number 30866F55Ro8C), two boxes of CVS brand bandages, a brown leather holster (a gun was not found) and other miscellaneous items.*

The report also said: *It is also noted that there was a ShopVac in Gerwing's garage. In the interview conducted with Gerwing by Inv. Novak and Inv. Florencio, Gerwing reported that his vehicle had been vacuumed. The contents of the vacuum were collected.*

The contents of the vacuum were forensically inspected, but revealed nothing to assist investigators. A BCSO report of July, 2007, said that the latex gloves purchased at CVS and drop cloths from Grayco were not recovered in the search.

It was later that Dennis confessed his fear that he might be arrested and sent to jail.

Dan Saxon said, "Dennis told me he was concerned he might be arrested, and his biggest fear was he might not be able to access his prescribed medications. I told him to get a 7-day pill container and fill it with his prescribed meds and, if he was arrested, he could take his prescriptions with him."

Saxon added, trying to comfort a very distressed Gerwing, "Don't worry, if they arrest you, I'll have you out of there within 48 hours."

Chapter 26

A First Love & A Beretta

It was big news when investigators searching Dennis Gerwing's home came across a holster for a pistol. Newspaper accounts reported the find and a call was received at BCSO shortly after that from yet another lady friend of Dennis Gerwing—Lesly Crick.

Lesly, Dennis's brother Fred said, was Dennis's first love. She wanted children and Dennis did not, Fred recalled.

"Dennis set her up in business—he wanted to marry her," the brother said.

Lesly said she had a platonic relationship with Dennis for 20 years. Her statement to the Sheriff's office was lengthy.

It said, in part, "When I saw the headlines in Thursday's *Island Packet* I decided I should read the reports handed out and available online...I about had a heart attack when I read the SLED report that a holster had been found at his (Dennis's) house. I knew right away that it must be mine."

Lesly, now married, related that she had moved from Colorado to

Hilton Head twenty years prior, and brought a pistol along for protection on her long journey. The pistol was in a holster. She had kept the gun in a box in her closet and had forgotten all about it until her young son discovered it. She took the .22 Beretta to a bank and rented a safe deposit box and put the weapon in it, out of harm's way. Told by a friend that a gun in a safe deposit box was not a good idea, she went the next day, retrieved the pistol, and put it in the glove box of her vehicle.

There, the Beretta remained until someone broke into her van. All the change was taken from her van's ashtray, and the glove box was open. But, the Beretta was still there. It had no serial numbers and no marks whatsoever.

Lesly then met Dennis Gerwing one night for sushi.

"Dennis said he knew an antique broker in Columbia that might want it (the Beretta). That was the last time I ever saw the gun. I never asked him about it, and I just assumed he gave it to the antique guy. I didn't even think about that crazy old gun again until I read the report on Thursday night and saw that they had found an old pistol holster that had a little strap that snapped around the pistol. The gun was my grandfather's gun on my mom's side, so it was very old. It was a black .22 Beretta probably about 6 inches in length. I don't even know if it worked," Lesly said in a written statement for the Beaufort County Sheriff's Office.

Investigators knew that a .22 Beretta was small, easy to conceal, and might leave little or no blood trail because of its small bullet. Twenty-two caliber pistols are known to be favored in gangland assassinations, and Detective Bob Bromage told the television series *Unresolved Mysteries*, "The .22 is highly suspicious because it doesn't leave a lot of splatter."

With searches completed at Dennis's home, and with Gerwing's attorney silencing him, investigators began to focus on Dennis's business partner, Mark King.

Chapter 27

Secret Recordings & Mark King

March 8 was a day marked with search warrants—Detective Bromage and other BCSO personnel and SLED Crime Scene Units, warrants in hand, went to The Club Group and found its offices locked and closed for the weekend. Bromage called The Club Group CEO Mark King. Could King come to The Club Group?

King responded by quickly driving to Sea Pines Center, welcoming Bromage and others into his suite of offices. Bromage asked King if he was willing to be interviewed. King responded without hesitation that he had no objection and led the way to The Club Group's conference room to be interviewed by Bromage and Viens. Asked at the outset of the interview to identify himself, King said he was the president of The Club Group and business partner of Dennis Gerwing.

Unbeknownst to King, Bromage was surreptitiously recording the interview. He revealed the secret record in his report of the March 8, 2008, session by writing, "The interview of Mark King was recorded surreptitiously with a Sony Digital Device." The Sheriff's Office said later that South Carolina law required that only one party need be aware that an interview is being recorded.

A portion of Bromage's report is as follows:

"King was asked his whereabouts on March 3, 2008. He advised that he had been at The Club Group until approximately 5:30 pm. He stated that Dennis Gerwing and Sha Ha (a Club Group employee) were present inside the business when he left on that date. King advised that he used one of The Club Group's housekeeping vans to move some furniture out of storage on that evening.

"King said that he drove the van to pick up some furniture belonging to his daughter and drove that furniture to his residence in Sea Pines, where they unloaded it into the recreation room. King stated that he and his son returned the van to the parking lot of the Sea Pines Center and then he drove Matthew back to his Sands apartment.

"King advised that he drove back to Sea Pines through the front gate and went straight home, where his wife (Leslie) had a meal waiting for him. King estimated that he returned home at approximately 8:30 pm. He advised that he did not leave his residence again that night. King suggested that he did not see John or Elizabeth Calvert on 03-03-08 at The Club Group."

Matthew King, Mark's son, was interviewed by investigators on March 12, 2008. The Sheriff's Report said:

An interview with Matthew King was done on 03-12-08 in an effort to corroborate statements provided by Mark King on 03-08-08. Matthew King stated that he moved furniture out of a storage unit with his father, Mark King, on 03-03-08. He stated that the move was unexpected because he planned on doing it the Thursday following. His father told him that he did not want to wait that long because he would be forced to pay another month's storage fee. He said that his father picked him up around 1800 in a company (Club Group) van from his apartment at the Sands. He stated that they proceeded to their storage unit, which is located behind the old Island Ford building in Bluffton, SC. He said they took the long way (278 Business) to Bluffton. He said that they loaded the large furniture and were there for about one to one and a half hours. He said that they left there and drove to his father's residence at 12 Oyster Landing Road in Sea Pines. He said that they unloaded the van and then drove the van back to Sea Pines Center to The Club Group's shop. He said that they dropped the van off and they both got into his father's Mercedes that was parked behind Sea Pines Center, and his father drove him back to the Sands and dropped him off. He did not see any unusual traffic while at Sea Pines Center and did not recall seeing either of Dennis Gerwing's vehicles. I asked him what type of vehicles Dennis drove. He replied that he believed he had a Jaguar convertible and a Suburban. He was unaware of the Toyota Avalon. He said that his father said that he was going home after he dropped him off.

One other note by investigators said "Chief (George) Breed of Sea Pines Security notified BCSO and advised that Mark King was issued a traffic citation by Sea Pines Security after midnight the night that the Calvert's disappeared. In following up, it was determined that the citation was issued in the early morning of 03-03-08, prior to the Calvert's disappearance."

King told the Sheriff's Office that he only handled sales and operations of The Club Group and that Dennis exclusively handled the financial end. King said he was not aware of any problems involving the Calvert's accounts and repeated that Dennis was solely responsible for those accounts.

The Sheriff's Office interviewed King, again on March 11—this time he was not alone. With him were Club Group property manager Bob Long and maintenance supervisor George Murray.

Meantime, Dennis Gerwing was upset that his home was ransacked by a Sheriff's Office search that left the ultra-neat Gerwing boiling. Investigator reports noted that searches of Gerwing's home obtained a toothbrush and two swabs. From Dennis's office the officers took a two-page facsimile. The report said the two pages referred to the disappearance of the Calverts.

Gerwing spoke with his attorney Chuck Scarminach by phone at 9:30 am on March 10, saying he would be staying at Swallowtail

Villas across the street from his business office at Sea Pines Center. He would be using a rental unit managed by The Club Group.

"I'll be staying there," he told Scarminach, while my home is being cleaned up," referring to the forensic search at 8 Bent Tree Lane. He gave Scarminach the telephone number of the villa. "Call directly back to confirm (the number). I'll stop by your office tomorrow."

Unknown to Dennis, by the end of the day March 10, there was so much circumstantial evidence against him that the Beaufort County Sheriff's Office was poised to name him as a person of interest in the Calvert case on the morning of March 11.

Gerwing did not indicate at that time that he was distressed or in fear for his safety. But, an investigative report following Gerwing's death, stated, "It is illogical to assume that the deceased did not realize that he was a suspect in the Calvert's disappearance…the deceased not only believed that he was a suspect but a suspect of a much more severe crime than larceny—murder."

Chapter 28

Investigators Bromage & Viens

D etective Bob Bromage of the Beaufort County Sheriff's Office was a native of Connecticut where he had joined the United States Army. His army tour ended in 1985, and he found himself in Bluffton, SC. Following his honorable discharge from the service, Bromage applied for employment with and was quickly hired by the Beaufort County Sheriff's Office. There, he excelled from the time he walked through their door.

Bromage was a recipient of the "J.P. Strom" award, the highest academic recognition the South Carolina Criminal Justice Academy gave. He had worked hard for that and numerous other recognitions, earning his stripes from the bottom up—he was first assigned to patrol duty on the midnight shift where he saw the seamier side of criminal activity.

His interest quickly mounted in the area of criminal investigation, and his competency was noted. After several months of training, Bromage was made a Criminal Detective in 1993. Highly intelligent and aggressive, he went on to achieve an Associate's Degree in Criminal Justice from Armstrong State College in Savannah in 1996.

Bromage continued to stand out in the Sheriff's Department and was given wide positive recognition by the Beaufort County citizenry. He was a Staff Sergeant supervising the Major Crime Unit and became the Traumatic Death Investigator in the department. There, he focused on cold case homicides and death investigations—accepting enormous responsibilities that required extensive casework. Bromage meant business, and within a few years, two cold case homicides were solved under his direction.

Bromage attended the FBI National Academy in Quantico, VA where he was immersed in behavioral science, management science, crime analysis, and constitutional law. Impressing his Sheriff, in 2006 he was appointed to the rank of Captain and assigned to the most significant challenges the Sheriff's Department encountered.

The death of Dennis Gerwing and disappearance of two prominent Hilton Head residents? It was not Bob Bromage's first rodeo. A top-notch investigator was taking on the case.

Bromage's associate, Angela Viens, was equally impressive. A native of Beaufort County, the tall blonde was a college volleyball star and a graduate of Coker College in Hartsville, SC. She joined the Beaufort County Sheriff's Office in August 1996.

In 1999, she was promoted to the rank of Corporal and spent the next 15 years in the Investigations Section, attaining the rank of Master Sergeant. Beaufort County liked Angela Viens as much as it liked Bromage—she was selected as "Southern Law Enforcement Officer of the Year" by the Hilton Head Island Rotary Club in 2005.

Viens was named lead investigator in the Calvert case and worked all facets of the criminal investigation. As Master Sergeant over the Southern Investigations Section, she directed and supervised daily operations. She was another "star" in the quiver of Beaufort County Sheriff P.J. Tanner. With Bromage and Viens on the Calvert case, Tanner had assigned his best of the best.

Chapter 29

Gerwing's Story Begins To Crumble

With suspicions that the Calverts were murdered, Bromage and Viens began a painstaking review of the veracity of Dennis Gerwing's statements as to where he was and what he did from the time the Calverts were last seen.

Hilton Head had two "US 278" designations. That fact would be important to the investigation. The William Hilton Parkway, Business US 278—was the older 278. It ran from the bridge onto the island and then proceeded past retail shops, restaurants, and gas stations.

The second US 278 was the Cross Island Parkway, built in 1998, to alleviate the congestion on the old business route, and provide much faster access to the island's south end. Motorists using this Parkway paid a toll, entering just after passing Spanish Wells Road on US Business 278, and exiting five minutes later after crossing the Charles Fraser Bridge that spanned Broad Creek. The toll-paying locals and tourists were deposited on Palmetto Bay Road, with a two-minute run to the front gate of Sea Pines Plantation.

At 7:28 pm, March 3, 2008, video and receipt records showed Gerwing purchasing Band-Aids with his credit card at the CVS pharmacy on Pope Avenue—the avenue that led to Forest Beach on the south end. He was recorded leaving the store with the Band-Aids and then returning approximately one minute later to purchase a box of CVS disposable gloves, with cash. He then exited the store a second time.

Dennis did all this within 45 minutes of his meeting with the Calverts.

Gerwing chatted on his cell phone during the time he was in the pharmacy. GPS cellular phone records revealed that Gerwing powered his phone off for at least eleven hours, avoiding any possibility of GPS detection as he moved about in a five-hour radius of Harbour Town—a radius investigators would target as the area where Gerwing might have disposed of two bodies.

Investigators carefully reviewed Cross Island Parkway video footage and records. Dennis had told them he traveled on US Business 278—the William Hilton Parkway the night of March 3—but the video records showed he used the Cross Island Parkway that night.

Gerwing had lied to the authorities.

His vehicle transponder registered in an outbound lane of the Cross Island at 7:28 pm. Ten minutes later, at 7:39 pm, Gerwing was recorded by video surveillance purchasing gas for his Yukon at Station One Convenience on Palmetto Parkway and buying a lottery ticket.

Sheriff P.J. Tanner said, "He lied enough in the first interview to give us ample time to run down a lot of stuff." Gerwing mentioned he was home when video surveillance and phone records established without question that he was, instead, buying Band-Aids and latex gloves at the Pope Avenue CVS Pharmacy, traveling on the Cross Island Parkway, and purchasing gasoline and a lottery ticket on Palmetto Parkway—not Business US 278.

Detective Bob Bromage told the television program *Unresolved Mysteries*, "His story was not going to hold up because he was on video surveillance at different locations buying drop cloths he conveniently left out of his conversations with detectives."

Chapter 30

★

Sha Ha's Journey

Sheriff's Office investigators pressed more shoe leather into their search, and on March 10 they interviewed Sha Ha, an assistant in accounting at The Club Group who worked closely with Dennis Gerwing. Sha Ha considered Dennis her mentor and friend. On March 3, she arrived at The Club Group shortly after 9:00 am. It was her first day back in the office after a four-week vacation with her family in China.

"It was a very busy day, and there was much work left for the month I was gone. I was in the office for most of the day," she recalled.

Around 3:00 in the afternoon, Dennis asked Sha Ha if she would follow him to Hilton Head Air Service so he could drop off his Toyota Avalon.

Sha Ha agreed. But, first, he asked her to follow him to his residence at Hilton Head Plantation. There, Dennis went in his house on Bent Tree Lane, staying, she said, for less than a minute. Sha Ha noticed no other vehicle in the driveway, and, once Dennis left his house, she followed him in her car to Dillon Road and the private air service near the Hilton Head Airport There, he parked his Avalon, got out of his car and into hers. Nearby was John and Elizabeth Calvert's parked plane.

Dennis told her he had friends coming into the air service later that night and he was leaving his Avalon for them to drive. Later, there was speculation that Dennis took his car to the private air service lot and left it there as a red herring.

Attempting to corroborate or disprove Gerwing's story, investigators obtained fuel logs from Signature Flight Support. The logs provided a record of activity during the time Gerwing's vehicle was at the airport. Tail numbers also were taken from the airplane fuel logs and crossed referenced through the Federal Aviation Agency register.

Investigators set about the tedious task of interviewing those who had come and gone at the private air strip. To narrow the effort, they eliminated several aircraft as either government-owned or belonging to large corporations. Seventeen planes then remained in question, and their pilots and passengers were identified. The Sheriff's Office proceeded to interview those parties as to any awareness they had of the disappearance of the Calverts. Some of those interviewed were aware of media reports regarding the case, but no substantial leads were developed, leaving unanswered who Dennis was expecting at Signature Flight.

But, did the Federal Aviation Register of those aircraft that had come and gone at Signature Flight tell the whole story?

In September of 2017—nearing ten years after the records check and interviews at the private air service on Hilton Head Island, the *Boston Globe Spotlight* investigation team reported that it had uncovered lax FAA oversight of licensing and registration. It even discovered people holding active licenses to fly or repair planes had links to terrorist organizations.

The *Globe* report found that one in six U.S. planes was registered in a way that made it difficult to identify the owner. The team found that the laxity favored so-called "bad actors" such as drug dealers or corrupt international politicians.

"People can use layers of secrecy to register their aircraft," *Spotlight's* Jaimi Dowdell told CBS News. "Those layers of secrecy are really attractive to drug dealers, criminals, corrupt politicians, and people with potential ties to terrorism," she added.

The FAA does not vet their registration records, the *Boston Globe* team said, because it does not have the resources to do so.

Could friends or associates of Dennis Gerwing have flown into Signature Flight with bogus credentials and aircraft registration obfuscated by layers of secrecy? It was 2008—if the FAA was lax in 2017, things might have been far worse in 2008.

The question is interesting, indeed. Could the person or persons responsible for the disappearances or the death have flown in, done the job, and flown out—their aircraft and identity disguised in layers of secrecy? Was the obfuscation so complete that the aircraft and those in the aircraft eluded the thorough search and exhaustive interviews by the Beaufort County Sheriff's Office?

Chapter 31

Drop Cloths & Latex Gloves

Sha Ha said she and Dennis Gerwing left Signature Flight Air Service and drove east on US 278 toward Sea Pines. Dennis asked her to stop at the Grayco Hardware Store on Business US 278—(the store subsequently moved to Palmetto Bay Road). She waited in the car as Dennis entered Grayco for just a few minutes, and exited with three drop cloths. Dennis told her he was doing some painting and needed the drop cloths. She thought nothing of it.

Later viewing of video surveillance footage at Grayco showed Gerwing walking into the store and purchasing three 9' x 12' heavyweight industrial strength drop-cloths that were thick and heavy enough to make ideal body bags. Gerwing paid cash.

Investigators later visited the Grayco store and observed that the material and size of the cloths they found in the store were identical to the three purchased by Gerwing and that they "appeared more than capable of containing a human body."

Detective Bob Bromage testified later that the drop cloths, "could be used for body disposal, body transport." Staff Sergeant Angela Viens said, "They could be used to protect surfaces from showing traces of blood."

Gerwing and Sha Ha left the Grayco parking lot, and she drove on to Sea Pines Center, where she parked the car behind the complex.

"Do you need help with those drop cloths?" Sha Ha asked.

"No," Dennis replied, "I can carry them myself."

The three-drop cloths and the box of latex gloves purchased by Gerwing were never recovered during the search of his home, business and vehicles. Investigators also looked for any packaging of those items and nothing was found.

No persons interviewed by the investigators were aware of any reason Gerwing would need drop cloths or gloves. He was not in the process of painting nor was he involved in any other activity that they knew of that would require such items. Some said he never engaged in physical activity.

Dennis retrieved the drop cloths from the parked car, and he and Sha Ha walked into the rear of Sea Pines Center and climbed the stairs to The Club Group offices. At 5:30 pm Dennis told Sha Ha that John Calvert was arriving. He instructed her to pick up reports from the Harbour Town Resorts and bring them to work the next morning.

Earlier the same day, Dennis called Judy Kirby, a contract employee of The Club Group who was expected to come by the office that day. Kirby's work required the use of the office computers.

Dennis's call was to tell Kirby the computers were going to be taken down for maintenance that afternoon at 4:30.

"If you're coming in, you should do it sooner rather than later," he told Kirby.

Kirby said she felt Gerwing was trying to keep her from just showing up at the office, as she was prone to do. After the call, Kirby said, she did not go to The Club Group offices at all on March 3, 2008.

Sha Ha felt also felt Gerwing did not want her in The Club Group offices the afternoon of March 3.

"I thought Dennis did not want me in the office during the meeting with John Calvert," Sha Ha told investigators. She left the office and saw John Calvert getting out of his silver Mercedes in the front parking lot of Sea Pines Center. Calvert was not carrying his briefcase. It was unusual, she thought, because he usually had the briefcase when meeting at The Club Group.

Later, around 7:00 pm, Dennis called Sha Ha at home and told her the meeting with the Calverts was over, and he was on his way home. He said the meeting had gone fine.

"I went to Harbour Town Resorts to find you, but you were gone," Dennis said. Sha Ha said she found nothing in the conversation that appeared suspicious and she went to bed.

The next day, March 4, 2008 Gerwing did not show up at The Club Group offices until 1:00 pm. He did not explain why he was so late. Gerwing swung by Sha Ha's desk and asked that she pick him up at his residence the next morning to drive him to pick up his GMC Yukon at the repair shop where he had left it. She did so on the morning of March 5, and they amiably chatted as she drove him to claim his Yukon.

Chapter 32

Gunfire On Calibogue Sound
& A Call To St. Barts

On March 10, 2008, Beaufort County Sheriff's investigators met with George and Louise Smith of 1856 Beachside Tennis Villas, 247 South Sea Pines Drive on Hilton Head. Here is the detailed report from the Beaufort County Sheriff's Office:

Mr. Smith stated that in the early morning hours of 03-04-08, he heard gunfire in the Calibogue Sound near his residence. Mr. Smith stated that there was a series of four shots, then one shot and then another. He reported that the gunfire was at approximately 0127 (1:27 am). He stated that he looked out of the sliding glass door and did not see anything nor did he hear any screaming. Mr. Smith stated that he was certain that it was gunfire that he heard due to past experiences of living in Kosovo.

Smith's statement to the Sheriff's Office read as follows:

At 01:27 on 4 March 2008 I heard gunshots as I was laying [sic] in my bed. The shots are believed to have come from the beach outside our balcony or from a boat on Calibogue Sound or from Daufuskie Island across the

Sound. There were either 6 or 7 shots. The first four or five were in rapid order. Then, a pause before another shot. Another pause, then a final shot. Everything in the area after the shots was dark and quiet. I didn't hear any voices or motors.

Could the shots have signaled the demise of the Calverts? Could the gunfire have come from the Yacht Basin? Or, were shots fired aboard a boat on or near Daufuskie?

There is no mention of investigative follow-up with Mr. Smith, a veteran of war-torn Kosovo, where shots rang with regularity, assuring that Smith would always remember that sound.

Meantime, Sea Pines Center resonated with sounds of retail activity in Sea Pines Plantation. There, upscale shops and Truffles Café drew locals as well as the influx of tourists that came through the plantation gates, mostly from June through August each year. High-end restaurants and storefronts offered expensive jewelry, massage, facials, and upscale women and men's fashions.

The shopping center encompassed several acres of pricey island land and consisted of a two-story complex in the middle with single-story shops at each end. Several hundred thousand square feet produced income through retail and office space rentals.

There, on the second floor, The Club Group offices were located. The Club Group managed the Sea Pines Center for Joe Fraser. Two longtime Hilton Head part-time residents and property owners, Ned Payne and Frank Fowler, would eventually own the shopping center in 2012.

Mark King would say of Payne and Fowler, "Both gentlemen have a great deal of experience and retail contacts that we hope can attract new tenants to the center." But, Payne, Fowler and The Club Group had a challenge—in 2012 the center had 23 vacant retail spaces, according to an article by Grant Martin in the *Island Packet*.

Dennis Gerwing knew Frank Fowler well. Fowler was, in 2008, president of the Harbour Town Boat Owner's Association. As such he regularly dealt with John and Liz Calvert—and Dennis Gerwing.

Fowler, an avid art collector and owner and investor in multiple businesses, was a seasoned sailor. He had sailed his yacht to St. Barts in early 2008. It was there that he first became aware of the disappearance of the Calverts:

"Whatever day it was that it hit the paper, I was in St. Barts and I received a call from Dennis telling me I would start hearing rumors that were totally untrue. He said the Calverts had disappeared and he had no idea what happened. He wanted to let me know he had nothing to do with it. He said he would talk with me later when I got home," Fowler said. But, Fowler and Gerwing never talked again—they would, however, exchange emails.

Following his conversation with Dennis, Fowler quickly went to his computer and Googled articles regarding the Calverts. He then called his son to ask what he knew. There was little to add. With just that sliver of information, Fowler sailed out of St. Barts and, days later, into the Harbour Town Yacht Basin.

So it was that, on March 9, 2008, at 5:44 pm, Dennis Gerwing said in an email to Fowler, who had just returned from the French West Indies, the following:

"Hi, Frank, welcome back. Sorry, u r coming back to this turmoil. The rumors r rampant right now, and we have a lot of work to do to try to overcome, not to mention the terrible potential for the calverts.

"Due to my meeting last Monday with the calverts, I may be the last known contact to see them, albeit we keep hearing there may be others. Therefore, as I told u on the phone, I am therefore a person of interest. Both mark and I have been interviewed, as well as my office, my home, and vehicles were inspected on wed.

"Last night our office, company vehicles, my personal residence and vehicles were actually searched under a search warrant for any clues, evidence, etc., including forensic. Based on the few items they took and results of black light, im hopeful that word will get out that these areas r clean. Nevertheless, this is just the beginning. The affidavit indicates that liz has used words like embezzlement, potential criminal prosecution, etc and that is the "motive". This is the area the fbi is focused.

"Mark and I met today and have decided as a first step, to hire a forensic audit firm who specializes in these types of reviews to address the issues she is raising, independent of me. We should meet this week to talk about including the marina regime in this review process, as I'm sure owners will be asking.

"My cell phone got confiscated lst night under the warrant and im therefore unreachable via cell. I plan to get a new number tomorrow. In the mean time let me know ur schedule.

"thanks dennis"

Frank Fowler replied on the same day at 6:18 pm. He was supportive of Dennis:

"Awful.........the rumors are flying. I put one to rest today........... rumor was 'embezzled over 100 K over the last 10 years.' I told the person, who, in turn told the person who had said it would be difficult since Pru had to audit to close and both Calverts and JR had made offers based on looking closely at the books less than 3 years ago. Hope it helps stop it. Sorry you are going through this. Maybe we can tlk? Off to NYC Wednesday until Tuesday for all intents and purposes."

Fowler's references to "Pru" was thought to reference Prudential Insurance, and the initials "JR" were taken to refer to JR Richardson, a principal developer and land/retail giant on Hilton Head.

Dennis replied at 5:18 am the next day, March 10:

"thanks...that's why we r hiring this special audit firm...trying to give credibility back to club group...also to try and answer the questions of fbi independent of me.
"Mark knows a person who works in this office, and he was going to contact him last night. Im going to have my staff start pulling all information today and try to bring them in this week to get started. Will do a press release indicating what we r doing. should know more at end of day. dennis"

Fowler replied at 9:22 am:

"wise......but expense that you shouldn't bear. You have to do it regardless of whether or not they are found to dispel the rumors."

Gerwing at 9:40 am:

"Exactly very expensive. ...ive made the decision to sell my house here, since the house in Columbia hasn't sold. Looks like Im going to need to generate some cash over the next 3-4 months and I have a fair amount of equity in it. Rotten timing but its got to be done."

Fowler, 9:57 am:

"move slowly....."

Fowler, 9:58 am:

"discount the house in Columbia since you don't plan to live there?"

Then, another email on March 21, 2008, at 4:06 pm. This one to Angela Viens from Frank Fowler:

"Subject: Fwd: Call me ASAP!"
Attachments: Call me ASAP!!!!"

There Fowler and Gerwing's emails ended in the official Sheriff's Office file. No response from Sergeant Viens of the Beaufort County Sheriff's is recorded.

What was so urgent? Well, 2008 was a while back, and Fowler had no recollection of that email.

"The Sheriff's Office never contacted me during the investigation, I felt like they didn't do a damn thing," Fowler said.

Regarding Mark King, Fowler said, "Damned if Mark didn't step forward and he's repaid, everybody. I don't know how you could be any more honorable than that. Dennis's brother Fred was the same way."

Chapter 33

★

Nude & Dead

An entire community was holding its breath and it was palpable. There was more to come, and events began to escalate on March 11, 2008. Novit & Scarminach's general counsel to The Club Group continued as usual and Chuck Scarminach needed Dennis Gerwing's signature on various documents to close a loan.

He called Dennis—could Dennis come by the next morning to sign the papers?

"I'll be there!" was the response from Dennis.

"Dennis was punctual—if he said he'd be there, he'd be there," Scarminach noted.

Except—the next morning Dennis was a no-show at the appointed time that Scarminach had requested for the document signing. Scarminach looked at his watch and eventually placed a call to Dennis. Dennis did not answer. Scarminach waited a while, and then put another call to Dennis's Swallowtail villa. He repeated the call, several times.

Scarminach, busy with a myriad of matters, shook his head and walked down the hall to the office of his partner, Dan Saxon.

"Dan," Scarminach said, leaning into Saxon's office, "would you see if you can run Dennis down? He's supposed to be here to sign those loan documents."

Saxon looked up from his work and nodded his head. Within a few minutes, he made his initial call to Dennis. He repeated the call several times during the next four hours—to no avail.

Saxon got up from his desk and walked to Scarminach's office where he told his partner he could not raise Dennis. They were both concerned—this was not like Dennis.

"Dan," Scarminach said, "why don't you go over to Swallowtail and see if he's okay—take Peter with you." Peter Strauss was a reasonably new associate with Novit & Scarminach.

Saxon and Strauss exited the law firm and took the elevator to the first floor where they accessed a vehicle and began the drive to Sea Pines Plantation and Swallowtail Villas, directly across the street from The Club Group offices.

They wound their way from the Plantation main entrance to the villas, and quickly found Dennis's car in the parking lot. There was no one in it. On the passenger seat, on the console, and on the floor of the vehicle, were personal checks, a Diet Coke can, and prescription receipts.

The attorneys accessed the front steps to the front door of Dennis's villa, pounding on it, to no avail. Saxon knew The Club Group managed the multi-unit, two-story residential complex and the company would have a key to the apartment.

Saxon called Chuck Scarminach and asked him to call The Club Group president Mark King. Unknown to Saxon, King also had been worried about Gerwing's whereabouts and had, earlier in the day, stopped by the villa. He rang the doorbell, "five or six times," and he had waited. There was no response.

King had looked in the windows of the units and had seen nothing. He came by the second time and, from the road, saw Dennis's car. He called the unit's telephone number, but there was no answer. He called several times more during the day, and time after time, the phone rang and rang—and rang—with no response.

Receiving Scarminach's call, King hurried back to Swallowtail with his Club Group property manager Bob Long where they met Saxon and Strauss. The group hesitated before using their key to open the door and rang the doorbell once again—waiting for five minutes as they repeatedly pushed the button that tripped the chime inside the villa.

No response.

King then unlocked the door but there was a privacy deadbolt lock engaged on the interior side of the door, barring entry.

Having no other choice, King and Long took turns hitting the door with their backs and shoulders and finally broke through. They entered a dark and silent villa that had all blinds shut, and called out for Dennis. No one answered.

They quickly moved to the second floor and saw an empty bed with what appeared to be a note scrawled on its bed sheet. Dan Saxon recollected that he looked down and there, on the floor, was a single pill. Saxon said, "I believe the pill dispenser was on the bedside table."

Moving on, they found the door to the master bath locked.

The attorneys and King called out for Gerwing, this time pounding on the bathroom door.

"Dennis! Are you in there?"

No answer.

The three men looked at one another in frustration and Saxon decided they should not touch anything and immediately leave the villa.

The men spilled out of the villa and into its parking lot.

What to do? What had happened?

Pushing indecision aside, Saxon whipped out his cell phone and called 911, reporting a possible suicide at 2899 Swallowtail. Then, they waited.

Gerwing, they knew, had just learned that an audit of The Club Group accounts had been ordered and that Dennis was aware it would reveal he had stolen over $2 million—or more— from entities The Club Group managed. He knew that the audit would show he had used the illicit funds for gambling and a myriad of expenses, including his debt for his yacht, *Big Girl*.

Had Dennis committed suicide? Was he killed? If it was suicide, why did he, just a few days before his death, insist on—seemed fixated on—making certain he had prescription medicines for the next seven days?

Chapter 34

★

A Bloody Bathroom

Emergency units from the Hilton Head Fire and Rescue Department came streaming into the Swallowtail parking lot shortly after
3:30 pm. They entered the villa, did a quick check of the entry area,
and called out Gerwing's name.

Silence.

The firemen and the attorneys rushed up the stairs of the two-story
structure and found the door to the bathroom also locked from the
inside. Captain Chad McRorie and Senior Firefighter Scott Layne of
Hilton Head Fire and Rescue hesitated, McRorie asked if there could
be someone inside the bathroom who might he be armed. The response was negative, and McRorie removed a small piece of the door
jamb adjacent to the door hardware. He then utilized a knife blade
to force the door latch, and slowly pushed open the door.

"Is anyone in there?" McRorie shouted.

No answer.

McRorie opened the door slightly—approximately ten inches—allowing him to look inside. Neither McRorie nor Layne entered the bathroom, but they could see blood—lots of it.

There was blood on the bathroom floor and the vanity and a white male subject was lying in the bathtub, covered in blood. A veteran in situations such as this, Captain McRorie told Layne and the attorneys to follow him outside.

McRorie quickly ordered the area outside Swallowtail Villas be secured and entry denied to all personnel. He then waited for responding police officers and told them what he had seen in the bathroom. Saxon said Club Group's Mark King was in shock. "Mark was sitting on a curb, his head in his hands."

It was 3:58 pm. Beaufort County Sheriff's responders moved up the stairs of the villa and pushed the partially open bathroom door completely open.

In the bathroom, they found Dennis Gerwing, nude, covered in blood—and dead. The bathtub contained no water. Strangely, Dennis's head was near the faucet. Ordinarily, a person would sit in a bathtub with feet at the faucet and back against the rear of the tub. Under Dennis's body, was a comforter and pillows. A serrated knife with a black handle was found near his right hip.

The bathtub was not large, but it was deep. Both of Gerwing's legs were bent at the knees; the legs splayed laterally over the end of the tub. The entire top surface of the tub was covered with dried blood, as was Gerwing's body.

The scene was indeed gruesome.

Gerwing had multiple ragged, large wounds. Blood had poured from his right inner thigh where a deep and vicious 4.33071-inch long horizontal cut had been inflicted. There were two wounds to the back and inside of his left wrist, each measuring 2.3622 inches in length, where a knife cut into his body. His right inner calf featured a cut of 1.9685 inches in length, and his left lower lateral neck had a horizontal deep gash 5.11811 inches long. It appeared as though his throat had been violently slashed.

Gerwing's right lower lateral neck bled profusely from a long and deep cut 6.69291 inches in length. It was astonishing—all those horrendous cuts. Dennis had been cut time and again. How could such violent thrusts be self-inflicted?

Blood was throughout the bathroom, staining the tub, the floor and sink. All the walls were heavily splattered—360 degrees of red sprayed wildly around the area. Barefoot bloodstain impressions were on the floor. There were 7-8 footprints with no visible arch, similarly sized, surrounding the bathtub.

Linear streaming small blood droplets were on the wall behind the tub, to the left of the body. They extended up the wall and above the tub for approximately 12 inches. The wall on the right side of the body and bathtub revealed a much more massive stream of blood droplets extending upward nearly four feet in length, forming an arc from the top of the tub near Gerwing's head, upward over a large picture and continuing farther upward toward the deceased's feet. A bowl of imitation variegated ivy was on the deck of the tub—eerily out of place in a room drastically altered from the time the greenery was placed there.

On the counter of the bathroom sink were a seven-day pill caddy and a prescription bottle. The bottle was empty. Near it was a plastic bag with assorted hygiene items and—a note—printed in blue ink.

The Coroner was called—the independent judicial official who investigates human deaths. The traditional primary responsibility of a coroner was to determine if the deceased did or did not die through foul play. In the case of Dennis Gerwing, the Coroner, Curt Copeland, sent his deputy, Ed Allen, to the scene.

Allen went about the business of recording all critical elements and facts surrounding the death and deciding if they could move the body from the scene without contaminating the investigation. A BCSO crime scene photographer was documenting everything. There was a conference with law enforcement authorities, and all were in agreement the body could be moved—then Allen began the task of collecting the personal belongings of the deceased and made the necessary arrangements to take the body to the morgue.

Some observers were not impressed with what they saw that day. One person who watched the Sheriff's Office access the villa said it was, "A circus."

The on-the-scene witness said, "It was not their shining hour. They ran up the stairs of the villa and threw open windows and shouted, "Throw me some booties and a body bag!" Other onlookers said, "The speed in which they brought the body down surprised me. Had they checked all the doors and windows?"

Asked later if anyone had contaminated the scene by entering the Gerwing villa before officers arrived, Sheriff P.J. Tanner said, "No."

Dan Saxon had another story.

"I don't recall if Tanner threatened to put me in jail, but that was certainly the implication. Tanner indicated that I had contaminated his crime scene and tampered with the evidence and that I needed to go write out everything Dennis had told me since this started," Saxon said.

Saxon was Gerwing's attorney and wasn't about to do that. He immediately sought a judicial opinion as to whether he had to comply with the Sheriff's directive.

"I don't recall if there was a formal hearing or just a meeting in the judge's chambers. I was at the courthouse for the hearing, but my attorney and Cory Fleming came back and said, 'We're done.' I was told that Judge Jackson V. Gregory said, 'So Dan is the deceased man's attorney and the question is whether the attorney-client privilege ends with death? The answer to that question is no, and Dan cannot be compelled to testify.'"

Considerable differences are apparent in the recollections of those who were there at Dennis's villa the day his body was discovered. And, debate continues to this day as to whether Dennis committed suicide, or came to his end in a more sinister way.

It *was* strange—if Dennis wounded himself in multiple areas before getting in the bathtub, it would seem likely he would have collapsed on the floor from such violence to his body. If he wounded himself *in* the bathtub, he would have had to get out of the deep tub, walk around, leave bloody footprints on the floor, and get back in the bathtub. That would be difficult to do, as he began to bleed out.

Benadryl was the only drug found in Dennis's bloodstream. Some said the amount was enough to kill him. Did he ingest enough of the drug to dent the searing pain of his first incisions? Could the high-dose of Benadryl make it possible for Dennis to continue to violently cut and slash his body?

Was there someone else present—someone wielding the serrated kitchen knife?

If so, how could that person exit the bathroom and leave no trace of blood?

Chapter 35

★

"Burn My Body"

An official report said Gerwing died the morning of March 11, 2008, between 5:00-9:00 am. The last time anyone spoke with Dennis was 9:30 pm March 10 when he called his attorney. What did he do between then and the time he died the next morning? There is no indication of what went on in his villa during that period.

But—there was that note on a sheet of paper on the bathroom vanity—with two droplets of blood on it. The note contained a long and rambling message. There were many abbreviations and misspellings. "Glow" is believed to be a security in which Gerwing invested.

It read:

"The answered questions: (1) Where is the money? The simple answer is its gone. (a) Glow hasn't $$$ recovered Stock mkt losses from yrs ago, including "Glow" which represents almost $900,000 in losses alone. (b) Haven't been able to sell in 2 yrs. In trying to recoup, I did the Wilmt house in 2001. That accts for $700,000 in refurbishment. (c) The most recent pressure was caused by my choice to fund Louis Ross' "SAV Mardi Gras Restaurant" made the mistake of guaranteeing the lease therefore

had to find extra $$$ to keep afloat. (D) Buying the "Big Girl" and living the "life style" also sustained rather than mitigated the problem. (E) While travel and kazam connex consulting will appear to also contribute, they are insignificant to the cause of the problem. For example, either (c) or (d) alone could have avoided the current focus. (F) Gambling not related. (2) Who did it? The acct transfers. I alone created + "benefitted" from the various "scams." No one else knew or should have known based on how it was done. (3) How to quantify? Besides the "follow the money" audit, The simple way is to balance all B/s Accts and then settle the I/C accts. All op revs + exp S/B already booked @ 12/03/2007. Follow the cash for 2008. This combined approach works. If one is ok w/the end result...Not necessarily the right approach on an ongoing basis. (4) what is the solution at this point. Suggest that one should do the accting outlined in (3) above and determine net amount owned by CGL then take DRG's major personal assets (i.e. Wilmot + HHP houses net proceeds big girl and his 24% interest in LCGI net proceeds as means of settlement. Any remaining personal or business interest value S/B settled as follows: Mark H. King 100%." (Here, three other names and percentages were written and then scribbled over. Investigators could not discern the names or percentages.) The note ended with these words: (5) Any prior will splits are hereby void"

The bizarre message was signed with Gerwing's name and dated Monday, March 10, 2008 @ 11:00 pm. It had a postscript.

"PS I have acted completely alone in all actions committed. I knew the risks of this happening and believe taking myself out of the game is the best way to move everyone as quickly as possible past all events. All anger should be directed toward me. Burn my body and dispose w/o service. It happened in SPC (Sea Pines Center) nothing happened at Bent Tree house."

Sheriff P.J. Tanner told media, "Dennis's notes gave us nothing. But, Dennis knew he was a suspect. He never took the opportunity to say he had nothing to do with it."

Dennis's brother, Fred, said Dennis did not seem suicidal when the two spoke after the Calvert's disappearance. He told *Island Packet* reporters Donnelly and Brownstein said that Dennis was concerned that authorities were jumping to conclusions about his involvement.

Dennis had, however, called his personal physician, Dr. Wayne Johnson, according to filed reports at the Sheriff's Office. That report by Sergeant Angela Viens said, "Dr. Wayne Johnson contacted me on 03-12-08 after learning of Dennis Gerwing's suicide. Johnson stated that Gerwing contacted him a few days ago and told him of what was going on. Dr. Johnson asked him if he needed a prescription for Xanax and Gerwing declined. He described his demeanor as 'stoic'."

Chapter 36

★

Murder—Or Suicide?

Investigators moved from the bathroom to the master bedroom. There, they found two empty water bottles, a watch and three business cards on a nightstand. Their eyes then focused on the sheets of Gerwing's bed where the top sheet and blanket were pulled down from the headboard. The writing was printed on the fitted sheet in blue ink. A pen was on the bed next to the writing. The note was not entirely legible probably due to the Benadryl Dennis had taken.

"...Slow way it's my wanting my body to wake up...3½ hrs. Jerk...brain keeps flashing w/a flash...the flash of a memory of old event...bright, like a computer photo type flash going off."

There was no evidence of any struggle, and no blood was found in the bedroom; no damaged furniture, no lamps overturned, no curtains slashed. Did neighbors hear any screams or shouts?

No.

There were no fingerprints found on the knife that had savagely ripped into Dennis's body. None. Further, a coroner's report said there was no indication the knife found next to Dennis's body had been wiped clean of any fingerprints.

No fingerprints. How could that be?

The report said it was primarily because of the coarse texture of the handle. A behavioral science analysis fueled speculation when it concluded that the absence of fingerprints "could be interpreted by some that an unknown offender killed the victim and left the knife to stage the killing as a suicide."

Statistics show that suicide with a knife is considered to be rare—guns are, by a vast preponderance, the weapons of choice by those who choose to do themselves in. And would it not be far too painful to stab oneself—repeatedly?

If somebody murdered Dennis, wouldn't there be multiple signs of a struggle? Wouldn't Dennis Gerwing have attempted to defend himself if he had been threatened? Wouldn't he fight for his life? Surely that would be the case.

But, Dennis's villa was undisturbed, save the blood-sprayed bathroom and turned- down bed sheets. There were no signs of forced entry into the home, nor was there any trauma suggesting Dennis was knocked unconscious.

The behavioral assessment read: "If homicide is to be considered, one would have to accept that the deceased passively surrendered, resigned himself to his fate, and while nude, waited until the offender located and retrieved the knife from the kitchen and cut him several times."

Research also showed, reports said, that people sometimes commit suicide with chainsaws and by setting themselves on fire—possibly exceeding the extreme pain of a kitchen knife and multiple, violent, jagged thrusts.

There was no evidence at the scene, or in later inspection of Ger-

wing's body, of sexual assault. Nothing indicated a theft had occurred. Gerwing's wallet, jewelry, electronics, and his vehicle were
not taken.

Chapter 37

★

A Change Of Opinion?

May 8, 2008—a SLED Behavioral Science Unit death analysis by Lieutenant Michael Prodan said a suicide note typically intends to convey information to affect the behavior of the recipients and may represent the "proverbial last word."

The report noted:

They are typically written in the moments just before the fatal act. If the time indicated is correct, it appears the deceased wrote the note soon after his telephone call with his attorney and within the estimated time of death. The reference to"taking myself out of the game" with instructions on how to settle his accounts, the voiding of previous wills, and the disposition of his body are consistent with statements typically seen in suicide communications.

The report continued:

As previously stated a major stressor in the deceased's life in the days prior to his death was the discovery and possible public disclosure of his 'inconsistencies' of the bookkeeping of the Calvert's company with the loss of hundreds of thousands of dollars and that the deceased was the last person to have been with both of the Calverts and was the primary suspect in their disappearance and most likely murder. When read with these factors in mind, portions of the note take on additional significance.

The portions of significance that were identified in the report were:

"The Answered Questions:" (plural past tense). This suggests that there are other questions and that he has not answered them.

Then—Prodan comments on what the note says about the embezzled money.

"Where is the money? The simple answer is, it's gone." The deceased does not identify who the money belongs to, only stating that it's gone. He qualifies the answer as being "simple" therefore there is likely a more detailed answer.

The deceased offers various explanations and justifications for the money being gone, none that are direct admissions to any criminality with the exception "I alone created and benefitted from the various scams."

"Gambling is not related." There is no reason to inform the reader of the note what isn't related (factors too numerous to mention are not related), therefore as the deceased makes an effort to mention gambling, his gambling most likely had some role in the loss of the money.

"It happened in SPC (Sea Pines Center, where the deceased's business office is located) nothing happened at Bent Tree house" (the deceased's home). The deceased does not identify what it is. Some may assume it is the loss of the money. But the loss of the money most likely occurred over an extended period. This statement is also written vertically on the paper, similar to the postscript and most likely is part of that postscript.

When reading in the context that the deceased was under investigation in the disappearance of the Calverts and Sea Pines Center was the last place they were both known to be alive, the statement has increased significance.

If one views the note as the deceased's admission, explanation and solution to the loss of the money ("it's gone", "living in the "life style", "taking myself out of the game is the best way…"), of major significance is the fact that the deceased made no mention of the Calverts, their disappearance, that he has been questioned by investigators, and that his home, vehicles and business have been searched at all (emphasis added). One would ask why he did not deny his involvement and proclaim his innocence when this would be his first opportunity to do so.

The report concluded:

The characteristics identified in this analysis cannot be considered in isolation, nor are they of equal weight of importance. The totality of the circumstances developed from the victimology, investigation, medical and laboratory reports, and scene examination were evaluated and compared to other homicides, suicides and accidental deaths.

The manner of death of Dennis Gerwing is best described as a suicide than either homicide or accident. It should be noted that this is an opinion and additional information may or may not result in a change of this opinion.

Then—a caveat.

Prodan wrote:

The conclusions are the result of knowledge drawn from personal investigative experience, education and research. It is not a substitute for a thorough well-planned investigation and should not be considered all-inclusive.

Chapter 38

Then You Can Kill Me

D ennis Gerwing's brother Fred was aghast at the photos of his sibling's death scene.

"The wounds on Dennis's body—when you look at them, it doesn't make any sense. It was a very vicious attack, much deeper than what you learn from reading the autopsy report. It's hard to believe anyone could stand that pain," Fred said.

He continued—

"The SLED reports said he probably took 12-20 Benadryl—he had 500 milligrams of Benadryl in his bloodstream. He had to be groggy at best and probably passed out. Why the coroner doesn't make more of that I don't know.

"I've got to believe there was some other party involved. I could see Dennis saying, 'I am going to take these drugs, then you can kill me. Make it look like a suicide.'

"The Russians may have wanted him out. They could have fed him the drug and made it look like others did it.

"It is a possibility that no one attacked him, he could have conspired with someone to kill him. I can see him saying, 'I'm not going to put up with this.' He knew he was going to jail.

"I talked to him by phone when all this occurred. I told him I would get on a plane and go to him. He said, 'No,' he did not want me to do that."

Chapter 39

★

Removing The Body

At Dennis Gerwing's Swallowtail villa, Officer J.P. Prusinowski was busy downstairs as investigators focused on the death scene upstairs.

In his Incident Report numbered 20080311-468—Prusinowski dispassionately demonstrated a professional's approach to a grisly job.

"I arrived at 70 Lighthouse Road Unit # 2899, Hilton Head, SC on 03-11-2008 in reference to a death scene investigation," he wrote. "The windows to the residence were locked. The downstairs back sliding glass door had a night latch that had been secured and engaged."

Dennis's brother Fred Gerwing had said, "I always worried that the sliding glass doors at the Swallowtail villa were never checked." But, Prusinowski's report specifically said they were checked and were found to be locked.

In the kitchen, Prusinowski found a Kendall Jackson wine bottle, one empty wine glass and two empty plastic Deer Park water bottles. (Pictures taken at the scene show a small amount of wine was left in the bottle.) In the sink were a plate and a fork. Beside the kitchen phone was a wallet with contents belonging to Gerwing, a pair of glasses, and a set of keys.

To the right of the sink, on the counter, Prusinowski observed a wine bottle opener with a cork in it. Next to the wine bottle opener was a plastic bag with a Publix grocery store receipt inside. A case of Deer Park water bottles sat on the kitchen countertop.

Prusinowski opened the refrigerator door. On the shelves were two yogurt containers and a potato salad container. He photographed everything.

Moving to the dining room, Prusinowski swung his camera into action, photographing a grey colored sweater thrown across a chair. On the dining room table was a binder labeled, "Swallowtail".

Moving to the second floor of the villa, Prusinowski sketched the bedroom scene while others measured the bathroom.

Prusinowski listed items of evidentiary value on his sketch.

A knife was found in the bathtub on the right-hand side of the deceased.

A suicide note was found on the counter in the bathroom between the two bathroom sinks.

"The deceased was found in the bathtub face up with his head toward the faucet end of the tub. The deceased's legs were up on the deck surrounding the tub at the opposite end from the faucet," Prusinowski wrote.

Prusinowski had not finished his work. He bent to the task of assisting Deputy Coroner Ed Allen with removing Dennis Gerwing's bloody body from the bathtub. Then, he and Allen carried Dennis's remains out of the bathroom, down the stairs and out the front door of the villa, depositing Gerwing's body into a waiting vehicle.

Officer J.P. Prusinowski had that day earned his pay, and then some.

Chapter 40

★

Seven Major Mistakes

Was there a comprehensive initial death scene examination that day at Swallowtail Villas? Were any mistakes made? The question was asked time and again as Hilton Head Island buzzed that this was a significant case—could local law enforcement conduct an investigation that was of the highest caliber?

Vernon J. Geberth, M.S., M.P.S.—a noted homicide and forensic consultant, wrote in the January 2013 edition of the highly thought of publication *Law & Order Magazine* that there are seven major mistakes in death investigations.

Here is a synopsis:

"Mistake # 1-Assuming the Case is A Suicide Based on the Initial Report (the 911 call at Swallowtail had said the caller wanted to report a possible suicide).

"If the case is reported as a "Suicide" the police officers who respond, as well as the investigators, automatically tend to treat the call as a suicide. It is a critical error in thinking to handle the call based on the initial report. The immediate problem is that psychologically, one is assuming the death to be a suicide case, when in fact this is a basic death investigation, which could very well turn out to be a homicide.

"Mistake # 2-Assuming the 'Suicide Position' at the Crime Scene.

"It has been my experience that when police officers or detectives hear the word 'Suicide' they go into what I describe as the 'Suicide Position.' Suicides are non-amenable offenses that are not recorded in the UCR and therefore are considered less important than other events. Without a doubt, investigators take 'short-cuts' when they hear the word suicide.

"Mistake # 3-Not Handling 'The Suicide' as a Homicide Investigation.

"According to Practical Homicide Investigation, all death inquiries should be conducted as homicide investigations until the facts prove differently.

"Mistake # 4-Failure to Conduct Victimology.

"One of the most significant factors to consider in any death investigation is victimology. Victimology, as it pertains to both suicide and homicide investigations, is significant in ascertaining motives, suspects, and risk factors. In suicide cases, this becomes paramount in determining Motive and Intent. Does the victim fit a 'Suicide Profile?' Was there any evidence of a marked depression or suicide intentions? Did the victim have both short and long-term plans?

"Mistake # 5-Failure to Apply the Three Basic Investigation Considerations to Establish if the Death is Suicidal in Nature.

"The investigator should be aware of three basic considerations to establish if a death is suicidal in nature.

1. The presence of a weapon or means of death at the scene.
2. Injuries or wounds that are obviously self-inflicted, or could have been inflicted by the deceased.

3. The existence of a motive or intent on the part of the victim to take his or her own life.

"Mistake # 6-Failure to Properly Document any Suicide Notes.

"If the victim left a note, and even if you are sure that the case is a suicide, obtain an exemplar (An example of the victim's handwriting from some document that was known to have been written by the deceased). This is necessary when later on there is a dispute over the classification of the death as a suicide.

"Mistake # 7-Failure to Take Each Factor to its Ultimate Conclusion.

"In order to conduct an efficient and effective investigation, the detective first concentrates on the mechanical aspects of the death, i.e., motives and methods, wound structures, crime scene reconstruction, bloodstain pattern analysis, the cause, manner and time of death, as well as other factors that provide clues to the dynamics of the event.

"The detective then accesses various sources, which can be applied to his or her investigation. In suicide cases the application of a 'Psychological Autopsy' might be useful in drawing conclusions but only if the information obtained for this instrument is taken concurrent with the event and not after people have formulated an opinion."

Were any mistakes made in the investigation of Dennis Gerwing's death? Opinions differed—but they did differ, and continue to differ for a decade following the discovery of a bloody bathroom at Swallowtail Villas and a corpse positioned not in the traditional way one sits in a bathtub, but backward, with his head next to the tub's faucet. Was there merely an assumption that this was a suicide? Were all bases covered?

To the dismay of some, Sheriff Tanner's team seemed to have made *none* of the "Seven Major Mistakes".

But, stubborn opinions were hard to change—there was no real way to tell, some said, if Mistake # 1 was made: *Assumption* that Dennis Gerwing's death was a suicide. After all, the initial call to 911 was to, "Report a possible suicide."

Chapter 41

Prayer Vigil & A Mysterious Note

Unaware of the gruesome discovery of Dennis Gerwing's body, but on the very day he was found, Laura Tipton was growing ever more concerned about John and Elizabeth Calvert. Tipton, marina operations manager at the Harbour Town Yacht Basin, decided to act—she announced a prayer vigil at the Liberty Oak in Harbour Town. It was the prominent location for summer concerts by Gregg Russell and the burial site for iconic Sea Pines founder Charles Fraser.

To some, it seemed appropriate to pray for the two well-liked, admired—and missing—entrepreneurs at the Liberty Oak. "You all prayed for rain in Georgia, and that worked," Tipton said. "We're praying for the safe return of John and Liz in hopes that will work, too."

Savannah's WJCL-TV news reporters Candace McCowan and Nathaniel Nauert were covering the vigil at the Liberty Oak when they learned of Gerwing's death at nearby Swallowtail Villas. They hurried down the street and began to video the exterior of Dennis's unit and the crowds that gathered to watch as first responders went about their business.

"What happened?" one onlooker asked another.

"They've found Dennis Gerwing," was the reply.

"Found him?"

"Yes, he apparently is dead, shot himself or something."

The news crew sought interviews with those spectators who would talk, and then hurried the short distance back to the crowd at the Liberty Oak, seeking additional "B Roll" video to accompany the station's story for its nightly newscast.

A light rain began to fall as the news crew headed back to their news van, parked nearby. Nauert approached the van and found a rain-soaked note on its windshield. The hand-printed note read, "This goes deeper than Dennis. Stay on it. Their [sic] are more people involved." There was no signature.

Back in the WJCL newsroom, the note "created a buzz." Candace Mc-Cowan called investigators on her return to Savannah from Beaufort County and told them of the note. WJCL began to percolate with exciting activity. Reporters and the station news directors were in full report mode.

Then—investigators demanded that the reporters who were hustling back to the television station bring the note directly to them.

WJCL newsroom management was told of the demand and, after consideration of whether to turn the note over at that time, declined to do so. The note was to come back to Savannah with the news crew.

An array of telephone calls followed, and WJCL made it clear to the Beaufort County Sheriff's Office that their investigators could come to the station after the nightly newscast or the next morning to receive the note. A WJCL staffer stressed later that in no way had the station acted irresponsibly.

The staffer contended reporters did not leave the scene with evidence, that someone wanted WJCL to know the information contained in the note. The reporter stressed that WJCL wanted the Calverts found, and that's why the station reached out to investigators to share with them, "even though we have had a few problems getting basic information out of them over the course of this nine-day investigation."

"The note was not the main thrust of our story we aired Tuesday night. It was one element that brought to a close a sad day on Hilton Head Island. Not only did one man die, we still don't have any idea of where John and Elizabeth Calvert are," WJCL said.

An anonymous Hilton Head Island resident seemed to put the possibly sensational story of the note to rest when he contacted the Beaufort County Sheriff's Office to say he had written the note and placed it on the windshield of the news van. The caller said it was an entirely innocent expression that merely urged continued investigation of the Calvert mystery. The Sheriff's Office Supplemental Incident Report of July 27, 2008, identified the writer of the note as Ned Nielsen.

As the Calvert case began to draw even more significant national interest, local media was joined on the island by CNN's "Nancy Grace," Fox's "On the Record with Greta Van Susteren", MSNBC, and ABC's "Good Morning America"—satellite trucks began to spring up like cell towers.

Major William Forbes of the Independence, MO Police Department and author of the textbook, *The Investigation of Crime*, entered the mix. He told reporters that some people might have a "natural aversion to hordes of media descending for a local lousy news event, but such coverage serves a real purpose." Forbes assured the *Island Packet* that such leads might not come in until months after the incident and media coverage helped keep the case alive in people's memories.

"You have to keep public interest up," Forbes told *Packet* reporters, Jim Faber and Tim Donnelly, adding, "To be honest, missing persons are one of the most difficult investigations there are."

The Beaufort County Sheriff's Office chimed in, saying, "Missing person cases in Beaufort County aren't rare, but it is rare when the missing aren't found."

Lieutenant Colonel Neil Baxley of the Sheriff's Office told the *Island Packet's* Jim Faber and Tim Donnelly that, in some missing cases instances, a person doesn't tell anyone where he or she is going. In others, the missing person returns and may not realize he or she had been reported missing.

Baxley said a few years before the Calvert disappearance a girl reported missing in Beaufort County later turned up touring with the music group, The Grateful Dead.

"She was selling T-shirts," he said.

Chapter 42

A Second Party Ruled Out,
But Debate Continues

The writing on the notes in the Swallowtail villa bathroom and master bedroom bedsheet were compared to known handwritings of Dennis Gerwing. A SLED Documents Examiner confirmed that Dennis had written both notes.

On March 12, a forensic autopsy and toxicological studies analyses were performed at the Medical University of South Carolina. The coroner's report said death occurred between 5:00 and 6:00 am on March 11. There was no evidence of blood alcohol content in Gerwing's body, but he had taken, at a minimum, 12-20 Benadryl tablets. One newspaper report also said blood pressure medication was found in the body.

Dennis's brother Fred had said, "Dennis had 1200 mg of Benadryl in his body at death. I spoke with two doctors who said that is enough to kill someone."

Benadryl aside, it was patently clear that a knife had slashed deeply into Dennis' right inner thigh, right inner calf, and right and left lower neck—and then he bled to death.

Investigators considered all possibilities but later wrote that the blood splatters in Dennis Gerwing's bathroom had no "void" that would be suggestive of a second person in the bathroom or near Gerwing at the time his wounds were inflicted. They further concluded that, based on the sheer amount of blood in the bathroom, it would have been highly likely blood would have been found outside the bathroom if someone else was involved in Gerwing's death.

Several forensic experts said slicing the inner thigh is an extremely rare form of suicide. "That's kind of an unusual place," said Dr. Werner Spitz, a Michigan forensic pathologist who has testified in high profile cases, including the Phil Spector murder trial. Spitz said in his more than 50 years of experience he had never seen a suicide caused by cutting the inner thigh. He said such a wound is more commonly executed in homicides or accidents.

Porter Thompson, the spokesperson for The Club Group, said a description such as that mentioned by the funeral director did not fit Gerwing. "He was not a troubled soul," Thompson said. "Most of the people I have talked to about this, and even some of the people close to it, are baffled by the method of Dennis' death and the adjudication of what it is."

Thompson, who knew Gerwing well, said of Dennis's death, "It appears to be a suicide, but a very draconian one at that. I think most of us that are contemplating our death would choose something less painful. I know Dennis well enough to say that he might not even know where his femoral artery is. He's an accountant," Thompson said.

Dr. Erin Presnell, head of the autopsy section of the Medical University of South Carolina in Charleston, SC, said, "With suicidal sharp-force injuries, you don't typically see any defense injuries."

She added, "You also could see different non-fatal, sharp-force wounds," where the person slices or stabs himself, but not deep enough to cause death.

Chapter 43

"Motivational Suicide" & More Questions

On March 27, 2008, a reporter asked Beaufort County Sheriff P.J. Tanner why Dennis Gerwing would have cut himself more than six times, suffering a gruesome and painful death. Tanner said it was "motivational suicide"—a term used by a second coroner's report hired by Dennis Gerwing's family—a family that obviously questioned the official suicide conclusion.

"What does that mean? Motivated by what?" the reporter asked, puzzled."That's what I was told," Tanner replied, referring to the second pathologist's report following an examination of Gerwing's body. "I can't give you a definition of that expression," Tanner added.

Newspaper reports following the "motivational suicide" statement said, "No definition exists for 'motivated suicide,' and it isn't an official term or description in the medical or psychiatric fields, according to several local and national doctors, experts, and coroners, who say they've never come across it before."

The chief medical examiner for the state of New Hampshire, Thomas Andrew, said, "That (motivational suicide) is by no means a diagnostic or medical term."

"I've never heard of that reference to a medical term or a forensic term," Dr. Kim Collins, professor of pathology at the Medical University of South Carolina, told the *Island Packet*. Collins and others contacted by the *Packet* noted that, after all, any person who sets out to commit suicide is "motivated" by definition.

Asked if that meant the phrase had some deeper meaning, the reply was, "Probably not."

Gerwing's death would be ruled a suicide. It is interesting to note that care was taken in the proper analysis of death with this language: "It should be noted that this is an opinion and additional information may or may not result in a change of this opinion."

Hilton Head Monthly asked law enforcement officials if organized crime might have played a role in Gerwing's death. They replied it was an outlandish theory—but one that could not be ruled out.

What kind of motives to kill himself did Dennis Gerwing have? In any suicide, the existence of, or lack of, a reason for the killing, is significant in determining if death is a homicide. No one could be found who held a grudge against Gerwing, but he was facing harsh charges and public scorn if he were found to be an embezzler. Would that have driven him to suicide?

Island gossip, rumors, and conjecture about Gerwing's demise ran the gamut from suicide to a Mafia hit and the question of whether Dennis was involved in some way in something far more significant than simple embezzlement—could someone have been using the Calvert businesses to launder drug money?

Oh, one more thing—Fred Gerwing later said, "I think a woman visited Dennis the night before he died. Dennis only drank red wine and the half-full bottle of Kendall Jackson Chardonnay and wine glass—suggests someone paid him a visit."

Chapter 44

Franciska & The Hit Man

Adding further to the enormous workload of the Beaufort County Sheriff's Office were some pretty unusual claims. Our Freedom of Information request revealed that Sheriff's Officer Michael Riley received a call one day from Staff Sergeant Brian Baird. A possible witness had been identified and interviewed about the Calvert's disappearance.

Sergeant Baird told Riley a woman identified as Franciska Zamfira had requested to speak with law enforcement. Baird met with her on March 26, 2008.

"She explained that she was involved with a person she identified as Lidge Randall Brock. She revealed that during her encounters with Brock he admitted to her that he killed the Calverts and that he was paid $100,000 for the job. She stated that he claimed to be the 'Hit Man", Baird wrote in his official report of the meeting.

This got some real attention, and Sergeant Angela Viens entered the Zamfira investigation.

Zamfira told Viens her relationship with Brock began after she moved to the Picket Fences Community in Beaufort. Zamfira's husband was enlisted in the Marine Corps and was on deployment for extended periods of time. Zamfira told Viens she had a relationship with Brock and that he was controlling. Zamfira said Brock told her his wife was unaware of their relationship.

Zamfira said she was fearful for her safety.

The investigation report said Zamfira told detectives she and Brock traveled together and, on one occasion, while they were in Florida, Brock had returned to their hotel room and told her he had just killed a man and that they had to leave the area. Zamfira said Brock told her he was a hit man and was connected. Zamfira then repeated the story she had given Sergeant Baird—that Brock said he was paid $100,000 to kill John and Elizabeth Calvert.

Brock showed the check to Zamfira—it was for $100,000.

Zamfira added that she saw Brock digging a hole in his backyard with a large tractor. She felt that Brock may have cut up the couple and buried them behind his house.

Zamfira was asked to take a Polygraph Examination. The report said, "No deception was indicated."

The investigators moved on—on to Lidge Randall Brock.

Chapter 45

★

Foreplay

With the information gleaned from Franciska Zamfira, the Beaufort County Sheriff's Office decided to conduct a sting—they placed recording devices to record conversations between Franciska and Brock.

The first session was unsuccessful—Brock made no incriminating statements as he and Franciska chatted.

Not to be deterred, investigators arranged a second meeting.

The recording device was running.

Sheriff's Office reports revealed that Zamfira and Brock began a conversation that caused investigators to lean closer to the speaker that deposited dialogue into an official file. The two discussed their relationship and then segued into some grave matters.

Brock told Zamfira, FOIA information shows, that he had killed John and Elizabeth Calvert. He said he pulled his boat up to the front door of their residence and entered their house and killed them. (The

Calverts did live on the water—they lived on the *Yellow Jacket*. But, Brock said he entered their "house," not their boat.)

In Brock's statement, he said he went on to tell Zamfira he shot both John and Elizabeth in the head. Brock said he was concerned, because of satellite tracking, of being caught.

The official report of the session concluded by saying Brock was saying things known to be false and that appeared to be a fantasy. The recording was turned off.

It was, however, deemed necessary by the Sheriff's Office to arrange one-on-one time with Brock. Sergeant Brian Baird had the job of setting up a meeting between Brock and himself—and Sergeant Viens. They met in Sergeant Baird's office.

Brock was first questioned about the $100,000 check that Zamfira said she had seen.

Brock had answers, and his responses were duly recorded by investigators, who wrote in their official report contained in the FOIA:

He explained that a man named Ed Wallace had given him the check as a return on investment. Mr. Brock gave Wallace $50,000 with the understanding that Wallace would double his money. Ed Wallace gave him the check as insurance on the return. Mr. Brock showed me that he still had the check and that it had not been cashed (check number 1113, drawn on an account held at Lowcountry National Bank by Platinum Properties, LLC).

Mr. Brock stated that Zamfira has been harassing him and will not stop calling him. When asked about his relationship with Zamfira, he indicated that he had provided financial support for her (approximately $70,000), has been involved physically with her, and that they had a business investment together that did not work out.

The report continued:

Mr. Brock stated that Zamfira is emotionally unstable and that he has power of attorney over her when her husband is deployed. He said that his wife is unaware of their relationship. She was involved with Ed Wallace before being involved with him.

Viens and Baird pressed on, asking about Brock's statements at Zamfira's home—statements they had recorded on March 27, 2008.

"Brock's reply, according to the official Sheriff's report, was:

Brock replied that Zamfira likes to play games. He said that stories like that are foreplay for her and she gets very excited. He stated that he tells her these things because it boasts [sic] her sexual desire. He said that usually she initiates the conversation and he plays along. She has said that she was a trained spy for the Romanian government.

What about the tractor and the hole Zamfira said he was digging in the backyard? The hole she feared would contain the cut-up bodies of the Calverts?

Brock explained that it was not a tractor—it was a tiller.

He said he had rented the tiller from EZ rentals and used it to prepare ground behind his residence for decorative pavers.

Brock said he did not dig a hole.

Would Brock submit to a polygraph test?

The answer was yes. An officer led Brock to another office where he took the test.

The "relevant questions" to Lidge Randall Brock were as follows:

(R5) Did you participate in the Calvert disappearance? Answer: No

(R7) Did you have anything to do with the disappearance of the

Calvert's? Answer: No

(R10) Do you know where either of the Calvert's are now? Answer: No

The polygraph administrator, Matthew E. Averill, reported the polygraph result in this manner in a document dated April 8, 2008: "NO DECEPTION INDICATED."

Zamfira also was polygraphed.

The "Investigative Polygraph Report" written by Officer Matthew Averill lists the following "relevant questions" used with Zamfira:

(R5) Did you lie about Brock telling you that he was hired to kill a wealthy couple who lived on a boat on Hilton Head? Answer: No

(R7) Did you lie about Brock showing you a check for $100,000 in February? Answer: No

(R10) Did you lie about Brock digging trench a [sic] in his back yard? Answer: No

Matthew Averill's report of March 24 says of the Zamfira poloygraph, NO DECEPTION INDICATED."

There was no deception noted on the part of Brock—and none on the part of Zamfira.

How could that be?

Sergeant Angela Viens said it often happened—two people can speak about the same incident, relate different recollections, and both pass the polygraph test.

How?

Because, Viens said, both parties honestly believe they are telling the truth.

Chapter 46

"Someone is Going To The Electric Chair"

On March 14, 2008, Master Sergeant Mike Riley went to the Calibogue Café & Trading Company in Sea Pines Center and met with restaurant owner Robert Alpaugh and his son Ryan. The senior Alpaugh told Riley he had video surveillance of Dennis Gerwing at the restaurant.

Alpaugh and his son Ryan both told Riley that on Friday, March 7, at approximately 5:25 pm Dennis came into Calibogue Café & Trading Company and came over to the Ice Cream/Bakery area where they were setting up their service bar.

"There was the usual greeting and friendly talk with Dennis, as he was a very good customer and we always chatted about various topics when he came in the store almost daily," Robert said in a statement he wrote for Riley.

"After a short period of this banter, Dennis announced that he was being asked by the authorities to put together a timeline of his whereabouts and wanted to confirm with my son exactly when he had seen Dennis the evening of Monday, March 3, 2008, at Sea Pines Center."

Robert described Dennis as a typical accountant— "Somewhat nerdy, quiet, facts and figures."

Robert joked with Dennis that the authorities were finally catching up with him after all this time. Unfortunately, Robert said, Dennis did not see the humor.

"Don't say that!" Dennis said. "These were my friends, and this whole thing is very disturbing and upsetting to me, and I was the last person to apparently see them."

Robert said in his statement that he and Dennis discussed his son Ryan having seen Dennis twice during the evening of March 3 outside their business while Ryan was taking a smoke break. Dennis and Ryan tried to figure out more precise times, but all they could come up with was Ryan had seen Dennis twice between 7 and 9 pm.

"I think it a bit unusual that the one time I saw you, you were going out back and then turned around and went out front when I saw you," Ryan said to Dennis.

"I parked the car out back earlier in the day and forgot I had moved it back out front," Dennis replied.

Ryan Alpaugh wrote a statement for Officer Riley that said:

"The first time I seen [sic] Dennis he was coming from the parking lot out front of my restaurant, going up to his office. I said hello to him and asked him if he wanted something, but he said no and unlocked the door and went in.

"The second time I seen [sic] Dennis I was out back and around the corner of Palmettos Clothing Store, smoking a cigarette. When I finished, I went back around the corner and seen [sic] Dennis come walking toward the back. I said, 'What are you doing?' He said, 'I parked the car out back.'

"I found this odd because I have never seen Dennis park out back and I was there, and his car was not there. I seen [sic] my server sitting on the bench out front of the restaurant, smoking, and I grabbed Dennis by his arm and said, 'I am going to sneak up on him and scare him, but he seen [sic] me.

"I watched Dennis proceed out to the front parking lot and I seen [sic] car lights flash like someone was turning off their car alarm. I did not see him leave in his car because I was talking to my server. When Dennis was heading out back, he did have a very strange look on his face, like he looked scared or something.

"Friday, March 7th, Dennis came in the restaurant. He asked what times I seen [sic] him on Monday and I told him it had been between 7 and 9. He talked about the two people missing and seemed real nervous and said whoever did this they would go to the electric chair for this and he said goodbye and left and that was the last time I seen [sic] him."

Ryan told his dad after Dennis departed, "He seemed disoriented and surprised when he saw me and his eyes were very big and he changed direction so quickly when he saw me."

Robert said Dennis, during their conversation, always referred to the Calverts in the past tense. "I asked him why he apparently thought the worst for them because he always referred to them as if they were gone."

"Dennis got very upset at that point and said, 'This is really a big deal, serious stuff, someone is going to jail for this, someone is going to the electric chair for this.'" Robert said.

"He seemed scared beyond belief, but yet my sense was he did not do anything, but that he saw or knew something. Maybe this was just my wishful thinking because Dennis was always so gentle, quiet and polite, and as has been written many times now, did not seem capable of violence," Robert lamented.

There was one more thing.

"My son also noticed a circular cut on his (Dennis's) hand and asked him what happened," Robert remembered.

"I cut it on a wine bottle," Dennis said, saying that was the reason for the circular gash. He added that the authorities had already seen the cut and had questioned him to their satisfaction.

"Dennis," Robert said, "was very upset that Ryan could not narrow down the times any better than he had seen him twice between 7:00 and 9:00 pm. Ryan explained that it was not uncommon to see Dennis at the Center at different times of the day and night, so he would have no reason to check the exact time when he saw Dennis."

"What do you want me to say?" Ryan asked.

"Just tell the truth," Dennis replied.

Chapter 47

Cadaver Dogs & Lagoons

On March 15, handlers of German Shepherds DeDe, Dino, Naudia, Cody and Simba of "Dogs South K-9 Search and Rescue", rushed to Republic Waste Management's Broadhurst Environmental Landfill in Jessup, Georgia, six miles outside the city of Screven, GA. Authorities had discovered that Sea Pines Center, as well as 20 counties in Georgia, and several Florida counties, sent their accumulated trash collection to the 2,500-acre Broadhurst Landfill.

The Sea Pines Center trash was loaded around the time of the Calvert's disappearance. Sergeant Joe Naia of the Wayne County, GA Sheriff's Office, said trash deliveries were "backlogged by about two weeks, which is fortunate in a way because that's about the time they went missing."

Twenty police officers from several counties converged on the site. They were daunted by the sheer size of the landfill but encouraged by the Sea Pines Center disposal timeline that Sergeant Naia had referenced.

State Police exposed cadaver dogs to clothing that carried both John and Elizabeth's scent. They then set about their business of search and discover. The dogs began to scramble through the mountains of debris, nostrils quivering. The search commenced on a Saturday night and concluded at noon on the following Monday. The sniff-search inspection found nothing. The same procedure was used in and around lagoons in Sea Pines and elsewhere.

Cadaver dogs were undoubtedly accurate, according to Sharon Ward, a cadaver dog trainer with Pacific Crest Search Dogs in Portland, Oregon. Ward said if a dog had the proper training in picking up a full range of human decomposition, its accuracy rate was about 95 percent. "So, if a dog says it's there, there's a darn good chance it is," Ward said. She added that. "The handler, especially a State Police handler, should know if a dog lies to him."

But, onlookers asked, what about all those lagoons on Hilton Head? Could a cadaver dog smell through water? The answer was yes, according to experts—the dogs specifically would search for the scent of human remains and detect the scent of human decomposition gases in addition to skin rafts. If a body was under water, skin particles and gases would rise to the surface, so the dogs could smell a body even if it was completely immersed.

Then, another discovery—some of the Sea Pines Center trash had also been taken to Hickory Hill Landfill in Ridgeland, SC. On March 20, 2008, the *Island Packet* said the landfill had not been searched "as of Tuesday." The authors could find no indication in any of the materials they reviewed that the Ridgeland landfill was searched.

If there was no search ordered in Ridgeland, why was that?

Chapter 48

★

Sheriff P.J. Tanner

P.J. Tanner joined the Beaufort County Sheriff's Office three days after his 21st birthday in 1981. Tanner was quick to tell folks that there had never been any question in his mind about what he wanted to do. Many years later and as the duly elected high sheriff of Beaufort County, he said, "I feel the same pride and resolve and enthusiasm today about serving as a law enforcement officer as I did then. As I have continued to gain a broader scope of experience, I have become even more committed to serving Beaufort County as Sheriff."

Tanner, a handsome, 6-foot, straight shooter, loved his job. But, he admitted time and again during the Calvert case that he was frustrated—it seemed to be a frustration far exceeding any he had experienced in his job before the disappearance of two of Hilton Head's most prominent business people.

The lifelong resident of Beaufort County shared his love of the law with his wife, Angela, an attorney and Magistrate Judge. They had been immersed in law enforcement for many years. Tanner began his service as a patrol officer and moved through the ranks from 1981 until 1995 when he transferred to the South Carolina Department of Public Safety.

There, Tanner served as a Protective Services Investigator and worked on the Special Weapons and Reaction Team of the Highway Patrol. Further duties with the state included stints with Drug Enforcement Liaison, Special Traffic Alcohol and Radar Team, and Environmental Protection and Enforcement in coordination with the United States Attorney's Office.

You name it, Tanner had done it: Patrol Supervisor, Boat Patrol Officer, Court Liaison Officer, Internal Affairs Officer, Swat Team Leader, Drug Task Force Commander, Southern Division Commander, and more.

Awards? There were plenty: Children's Health, Support of Narcotic Law Enforcement, Career Excellence, Warriors Training Warriors, Sun City Safety & Service, Keepers of The Flame, Expertise and Leadership of Service, Diamond Pharmacy Services, Part of Your Team, Special Deputy United States Marshal for South Carolina, Partnership for Public Safety, Republican Party Local Government, Citizens Opposed to Domestic Abuse, and, oh yes, Sheriff of the Year in South Carolina.

Tanner was not a man to sit around.

A Republican with a list of awards and memberships in county and state activities as long as both his arms, Tanner was well-known and well-liked in South Carolina. He decided in 1997 that he would run for Sheriff of Beaufort County. He won his race and served his first term from 1999-2003. He was re-elected in 2003, serving through 2007. He would go on, winning four 4-year terms as Sheriff.

But, it was that election to his third four-year term that brought him face-to-face with March 2008 and the disappearance of John and Elizabeth Calvert. The third term and those calamitous days of, first, the mysterious Calvert disappearance, and then the apparent suicide of Dennis Gerwing—along with the speculation that Gerwing had not taken his life but had been murdered in a gruesome and bizarre manner, would have been enough to test the ultimate professional—and Tanner was just that.

Photo: Hilton Head Monthly

Photo: Sea Pines Center

John and Elizabeth Calvert

Photo: Jonathan Dyer, Island Packet

Sheriff's officers with the Calvert's yacht *Yellow Jacket*.

Back stairs at Sea Pines Center. ★
Gerwing's office top right of photo.

The Club Group office door at right;
elevator on left.

Nancy Barry

Dennis Gerwing

Sheriff P. J. Tanner

Detective Bob Bromage
Now Captain

Detective Angela Viens
Now Lieutenant

Chief Deputy Michael M. Hatfield
Provided FOIA information.

Beretta Holster found at Dennis Gerwing's home.

1934 Beretta like the one
in Dennis's possession.

Dennis Gerwing & John Calvert
at the Yacht Hop 2006.

Charles A. Scarminach
Attorney at Law

Daniel A. Saxon
Attorney at Law

Half full bottle of Kendall Jackson Chardonnay and wine glass in Swallowtail villa in Sea Pines.

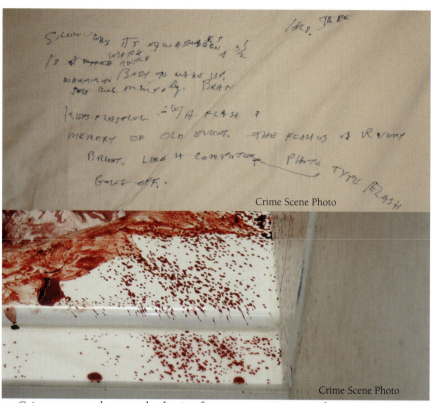

Crime Scene Photo

Crime Scene Photo

Crime scene photos: clockwise from top writing on sheet in Dennis's villa, blood spatters in bathroom, bloody footprints on floor and suicide note.

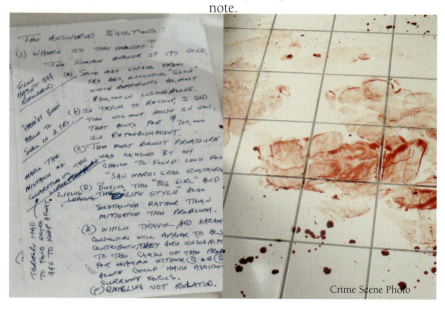

Crime Scene Photo

Steak knife found beside Dennis Gerwing's body in bathtub at Swallowtail villa. Adult videos found in Gerwing's Avalon & the suicide note signed and dated. All crime scene photos.

Alligators at Savannah National Wildlife Refuge.

Yacht *Spirit of Harbour Town* used for Calverts' memorial service
Sunday, September 7, 2008.

Calvert bench in Six Oaks Cemetery in Sea Pines.

Chapter 49

Ninjas, Cocaine & "A Bloody Mess."

September 7, 2017, Sheriff P.J. Tanner, Detective Bob Bromage and Sergeant Angela Viens sat with authors Ryan and Ovens in a conference room at the Hilton Head Island Sheriff's Office. The three law enforcement officials gave one and one-half hours of their time to discuss John and Elizabeth Calvert and Dennis Gerwing.

The Sheriff's Office officials' time was always valuable, but even more so on that day because Hurricane Irma was on the move through the Caribbean with forecasts contending the Category Five storm was on a path to pummel Beaufort County. Tanner himself was just a few hours away from a significant public briefing on preparedness activities his office would implement.

There was no doubt on that day that job number one for Tanner and his deputies was to prepare to provide emergency services to the people of Beaufort County. But, at the same time, he, Viens, and Bromage obviously wanted to take time to review the Calvert case, because the open file remained of high importance to them.

And—they also wanted to make sure those stories of Ninja Warriors taking Dennis Gerwing out, and other ridiculous rumors surrounding the case were balanced with the impartial investigation of law enforcement professionals. Tanner found the media coverage of the case somewhat amateur.

"Lots of things the media never picks up on," he said.

For instance?

The Sheriff's Office brought a medical expert to Swallowtail Villas where Dennis died—the expert was a wheelchair-bound medical pathologist.

"He was in a wheelchair, and it was all filmed by local media," Tanner said.

Tanner, Bromage and Viens said they were amazed that no one asked, as a lift was used to raise the doctor and his wheelchair into the villa, "Who's the guy in the wheelchair?"

Had they asked, Tanner said, they would have learned that the Sheriff's Office had brought learned pathologist Roger Sorg to the death scene as an extra step in establishing Gerwing's cause of death.

Sorg's findings, dated 03/11/2008, said, in part:

Manner of Death: Apparent Suicide (Pending MUSC forensic autopsy)

Immediate Cause of Death: Multiple self-inflicted lacerations with massive hemorrhage

Contributory Findings: Two suicide notes (white single sheet of paper & bottom bed sheet)

It was signed:

Roger J. Sorg, DO
Pathologist, Deputy Coroner
March 15, 2008

"There was never any question it was a suicide," Tanner said. "Sorg did an independent review, and two other pathologists agreed—Dennis died by his own hand."

But, the Sheriff said, "That was too cut and dried for media, and they wanted to throw some mystery into it—cocaine lords, and so on." Tanner and Bromage smiled at the exaggerations and rumors that spread around the suicide.

Tanner said the reality was, "When he left suicide notes he never took the opportunity to say he had nothing to do with it."

A profiler from SLED agreed, saying there was a lot of information in Dennis's notes, but at no time did he ever disengage himself in any way.

And what about the Calverts? Were they murdered?

"The reality is, this is a missing person case, not a double homicide." Tanner said, "When it comes down to bodies, that's not something we have."

No third party?

"We don't know. There were multiple accounts of Dennis Gerwing as, some said, quiet, shy, not physically fit—but, on the other side, he reportedly had a temper. John and Elizabeth were smaller size people. Have you ever moved furniture? There is a lot that can be done with an adrenalin rush," Tanner said.

Asked if the death scene was violated with the presence of multiple persons at the scene, Tanner said no—disagreeing with attorney Dan Saxon who said Tanner had accused him of contaminating his crime scene and tampering with the evidence.

What about the knife found beside Dennis's body—why couldn't the knife have provided fingerprints?

177

"It was a bloody mess," Bromage said.

Had the Sheriff's Office heard of a *Journal of Forensic Sciences* article about the use of Vacuum Metal Deposition to develop sebaceous fingermarks from non-porous substrates—a new way that might be used on the rough handle of the knife found beside Dennis Gerwing's body? The knife showed no fingerprints and no evidence it had been wiped clean.

No, they had not heard of that.

"That might be something for SLED to look at," Bromage said.

Was there a guest in Gerwing's villa the night before he died?

"Maybe, who would know?" was the reply.

Sergeant Viens said, "I have a three-ring binder of 'tips'—when I get a call from a local who sounds relevant, it is always followed up."

The authors asked, "We are told there were seven people who took the polygraph test. Did a married couple, Laura and Rob Merrill, named in investigative reports, take a polygraph test? Did Laura fail her test?"

The response was that Laura did not take the test, her husband, Rob, did.

"Did anyone fail the polygraph tests?" the investigators were asked.

No one failed, was the response.

A few final questions to Sheriff Tanner:

"If Dennis had lived, been arrested and charged with the murders of the Calverts, would you have had enough evidence to convict him?"

Tanner: "I'm not a lawyer, but based on what we had it would be circumstantial. That would not get a guilty verdict in a courtroom in a case of this magnitude. It would be difficult to get a jury to indict. There was a lot of circumstantial evidence Angela gathered during the first 48 hours that he was absolutely a person of interest. The problem was, he killed himself."

Tanner had said in 2008 he believed Dennis acted alone in the Calvert case, but that was something they were, "still looking at."

In September, 2017 Tanner said that still rang true—they were always looking at a possible second party or parties.

Tanner also said in 2008 that it would be difficult to get anyone to come forward in the case because they very likely would be considered a co-conspirator.

Was that still true in 2017?

Tanner said, "Still true. The theory is if we had someone who had independent knowledge of what we had closely assimilated with Dennis they would become a person of interest. If you come in and fully cooperate, we can vet you…if you come in and tell a little bit of the story you become a person of interest."

The Sheriff's Office found no drug involvement, no organized crime activity and no evidence of money laundering. Asked if the Calverts' bodies could have been tossed into lagoons on properties that The Club Group managed in Georgia, the answer was that the lagoons at those locations were extremely shallow and would not provide cover for the bodies.

Further, they knew of no "gambling houses" in Wexford Plantation.

In short, the Sheriff's Office said the case of the Calvert disappearance remains open, and anyone with any information about the Calverts should call 1·888·CrimeSC. The anonymity of the callers would be protected.

The long-term Sheriff must have grown weary of all those rumors and speculations and the Monday morning quarterbacks who second-guessed his direction of the case, not to mention those who said, over cocktails at the Sea Pines Country Club, that he was in over his head.

And then, there were those nationally-known reporters that had landed on Hilton Head's shores to report on the case.

Then there were those pesky local reporters who seemed to follow every move of the Sheriff's Office and were knowledgeable about the situation.

Chapter 50

Brownstein & Donnelly Dig Deeper

" The disappearance of two prominent Hilton Head Island people
was a big deal. It was surreal to see cable news trucks lined up at
the Sea Pines Welcome Center," *Island Packet* reporter Tim Donnelly
said. "Here we were, in a usually very sleepy little town, six weeks
before the Heritage PGA Tournament. And underneath the calm,
there was this awful crime happening."

The *McClatchy*-owned newspaper had freed Donnelly and Brownstein
to devote all their time to following the Calvert case. "It was pretty
easy, on such a small island, to follow police wherever they went. We
were behind hedges at Swallowtail Villas and Sea Pines Center when
the Sheriff's Office was investigating the scene where the Calverts
were last seen, and the site of Gerwing's assumed suicide," Brownstein said.

The two crouched behind bushes and watched as police cordoned
off Gerwing's Swallowtail villa—Sheriff P.J. Tanner and Detective Bob
Bromage going in and out of the villa, Fourteenth Judicial Circuit
Solicitor Duffie Stone arriving, having been summoned to the scene
as a known friend of Gerwing. *Island Packet* readers hurried for their

newspaper the next day to read that which Brownstein and Donnelly had written.

Brownstein and Donnelly were the island's Woodward and Bernstein. They were relentless and undaunted by official restrictions. The day after Gerwing's body was removed from the Swallowtail villa, Brownstein and Donnelly went to that villa and convinced a cleaning person to allow them entry.

"We talked with a man who was cleaning the place and got into Gerwing's villa the very next day after the alleged suicide. We saw no blood—it had been cleaned up. There was no evidence of a struggle and, really, little evidence that anyone had been there," Brownstein said. "We went through the whole place and paused in the bathroom, which had been cleaned but was still quite eerie, given the gruesome scene that had transpired the day before," Brownstein recalled.

Strange indeed that authorities allowed the Swallowtail villa to be scrubbed clean the day after Dennis Gerwing's gruesomely lacerated body was discovered. Why would the Beaufort County Sheriff's Office not have cordoned off the scene for days, allowing for subsequent inspection of the death site as the investigation continued? Did the quick ruling of "suicide" justify an "all clear" that allowed scrub brushes and mops to wipe away blood, fingerprints, and other forensic evidence? Was critical evidence destroyed?

A Fox videographer followed Dan Brownstein as he covered the story. The Fox representative simply attached himself to Brownstein, who seemed to know everything about the case. This was becoming the norm—national media that flocked to and from the island in spurts clung to both Donnelly and Brownstein, recognized local reporters, who were in constant touch with developments. They unapologetically used Brownstein and Donnelly's research and legwork.

Good Morning America said that national reporters were giving adulation to Brownstein and Donnelly's reporting and the morning news and entertainment program came calling to the *Packet* newsroom.

"They wanted to film Tim and me, and they posed us in front of a computer where we pretended to converse regarding the Calvert story," Brownstein said, shaking his head. "We were doing Fox and MSNBC live shots almost every hour for a couple of days. It was weird. They were not doing any reporting; they were relying on us," he said.

Brownstein said he was lying in bed in Beaufort at 6:00 am when MSNBC, "called and woke me up. They were supposed to interview Tim, but they couldn't locate him, so they called me, and I did the interview. Then, Geraldo Rivera's brother Greg was sent down to Hilton Head, and I was interviewed as we walked around the Yacht Basin. There was lots of interest."

Brownstein and Donnelly were unfazed by their instant celebrity. They were serious about their work and not interested in any carnival atmosphere that seemed to be building around the story. They followed up on all rumors. One said Gerwing and The Club Group controlled liquor sales on the Harbour Town golf course during the Heritage Tournament and Gerwing was seen walking around the grounds with bags full of money. The reporters also zoned in on rumors of Dennis's gambling habit and his fondness for area strip bars.

Strip bars?

Tim Donnelly decided to check that one out. He drove through bright afternoon sunshine to the island's "Club Paradise" where bright lights advertised girls, girls, girls, and drinks. Tim had never been to a strip bar, and he knew most patrons would choose nighttime to visit. But, he forged ahead, opening the door to the club and walking in.

Daylight disappeared behind him, and he adjusted his eyes to the darkness and his ears to the thumping boom of loud music. A pole dancer was going through the motions as he walked to the bar. Fascinating, Tim thought to himself, being in a strip joint in the middle of the day.

"Yes?" said a man behind the bar, eying Tim as the only customer in the club at 2:00 in the afternoon.

"Tim Donnelly," the young reporter yelled by way of introduction as the music seemed even louder, "I was wondering if you could tell me if Dennis Gerwing ever came in here?"

"You a cop?"

"No, a reporter for the *Packet*."

"Okay, big story, huh?"

"You might say so; they found Dennis dead, guess you know."

"Yep, saw that. Dennis did come in here, from time to time."

"Anything unusual happen?"

"Nope, just a regular run of the mill customer," was the reply.

Donnelly and Brownstein continued to dig. They followed reports of a Russian girlfriend Dennis supposedly had. She was said to work at the Hinoki Sushi restaurant on New Orleans Road. Off they went to Hinoki where they gave the woman's name to the manager, telling him they were pretty sure Gerwing had been dating his Russian waitress.

"Does she still work here?" they asked.

"No, she quit some time ago," was the reply.

"They were a bit cagey about discussing her with us," Brownstein later recalled, smiling.

On the reporters went to posh Wexford Plantation to follow up on rumors of a gambling ring that met at a multi-million-dollar home in the inland marina development where man-made locks allowed plantation yacht owners to move their expensive yachts directly into Broad Creek without worrying about the changing tides. At Wexford, supposedly, Russian women connected with the Russian Mafia "worked" the gambling parties.

The reporters found no one who knew of such a setup and saw nothing to confirm the rumors of a gambling network.

Day in and day out, the two reporters followed the cops. Each time a new detail of the story leaked out, there were Brownstein and Donnelly, peppering questions. Sheriff Tanner was playing the whole thing close to his vest and only when throngs of national reporters came knocking on his door did Tanner decide to hold regular press briefings.

"We had done a whole story about casting doubt on the investigation. I interviewed a couple of forensic experts and Tanner accused me privately of writing *Nancy Drew Mysteries*. He is a strong personality and, being local reporters, we had a closer relationship with him than did the national media and we had exchanges like that," Brownstein said.

Donnelly and Brownstein fired lots of questions at Tanner's press briefings, and at one such get-together, the Sheriff fired back, this time publically accusing Brownstein of writing *Nancy Drew Mysteries*, pricking Dan on national television. To Dan, it felt good. He was doing his job.

"We always sensed the Sheriff's Office was overwhelmed by the case. They had to send a lot off to Columbia. The Sheriff's Office was not very transparent, and we found them very condescending—standoffish. In the beginning, there was an overwhelming interest in the story, and they did not reveal much information. They became more informative as time passed and finally did release a synopsis of the investigation and some of the details of the suicide notes," Brownstein said.

"We found some things I don't think authorities ever checked out," Brownstein added.

Like what?

"Well," Brownstein mused, "there was the island boat captain who told us he saw a boat in Harbour Town very late, totally dark, the night of the Calvert's disappearance. He said the boat's pilot was obviously unfamiliar with Calibogue Sound and almost hit a sandbar."

Chapter 51

A Shadowy Apparition

Captain Ray Morris came to Hilton Head Island from Greensburg, Pennsylvania, twenty minutes from Latrobe, the home of Arnold Palmer, winner of the first Heritage PGA Golf Tournament at Harbour Town Golf Links. Ray was not an Arnold Palmer on the links, but he was recognized as a superlative man on the water.

Not only that, Ray had played drums back in the day with Tommy James and the Shondells. It was the 1960s. Morris, considered by all to have a highly refined sense of humor, maintained a full head of brown hair and the ladies found him very handsome. It was good to be Ray.

Love of sailing and boating, in general, drove Captain Ray to earn his "Master Near Coastal" license to captain passenger vessels. He became a ferryboat captain who crisscrossed Calibogue Sound thousands of times, ferrying passengers to Haig Point on Daufuskie, the small island that time had forgotten.

Well, not all that forgotten—there had been those mammoth developments that deposited hundreds of millions of dollars in several resorts on Daufuskie, and there were those hotel size homes. But—Daufuskie did maintain its remoteness—one needed a boat to access the island. And, it retained its sense of history—native island Gullah people lived there—people who still spoke the Gullah dialect. Dirt roads ran throughout the island, and a local real estate salesman persisted in telling tourists that "Daufuskie" was Gullah for "Duh first key." Daufuskie is actually an Indian name meaning "pointed feather." And it was on Daufuskie that Lowcountry author Pat Conroy taught at a one-room school—an experience he would turn into the best-selling novel, *The Water is Wide*. The tiny schoolhouse still proudly stood on the island, now marked as an historic site in South Carolina. Daufuskie also boasted of having some residents with famous names, one being John "Cougar" Mellencamp.

Captain Ray Morris worked the night shift on the Haig Point ferry. He liked the night shift—it was quiet, and during the sub-tropical South Carolina nights Ray thanked the soft summer winds that cooled his face and calmed his soul. It was far better than meditation.

On one of those shifts—March 4, 2008 at 3:45 am—to be exact, Captain Ray said he was taking the ferry over to the fuel dock at Harbour Town to pick up passengers early that morning. He had made the crossing in the dark many times, but this venture was blacker than most. Not a problem, Captain Ray knew Calibogue Sound like the back of his hand. This crossing would be different, however, as he would see something he had never seen in over thirty years on the water.

There was another boat at the fuel dock, and it was manned. It was strange, Morris thought, because he had never seen such a large boat seemingly ready to cast off at that time of morning. Surely the crew was heading for the Intracoastal Waterway, but, one rarely ventured out into the Intracoastal in darkness. That would be crazy and suicidal. Every boat captain knew that, especially if the pilot did not realize the hazards there. Captain Ray had never seen this particular boat in Calibogue Sound or Intracoastal Waterway. He silently mused as to whose boat it was, and from where it came, and where it might go.

"There were two crew, both men, on the boat. They looked to be in their 40s or early 50s," Morris said. Captain Ray squinted and focused, but he could not make out the name on the big boat—too far away. Morris was, however, able to see lots of activity—it looked as though she was ready to leave the dock.

"The boat had sliding glass doors where the two men were standing. I smiled at the two and waved, but they didn't crack a smile or raise a hand. The whole thing was odd because the only people I ever saw at that time of the morning were my passengers."

Captain Ray went about his business and boarded his early morning passengers as they arrived. Then, back across Calibogue Sound to Daufuskie Island that beckoned with its iconic lighthouse, as it had for generations before Ray Morris's time.

As the water pounded the ferry, Captain Ray's thoughts turned once more to the rather mysterious boat he had seen docked at Harbour Town in the middle of the night.

At 5:30 am Morris left Daufuskie once more, after picking up a passenger bound for Hilton Head Island's airport. As he motored back to the fuel dock he saw that the big boat he had seen earlier was gone—but Ray knew it had not crossed Calibogue Sound, he would surely have seen the vessel because their paths would have crossed. Morris turned his attention toward the Sound. The strange and unfamiliar craft could only have set course for the Intracoastal Waterway.

"You know," the longtime Captain said, relating his experience, "no one ever ventures out on the Intracoastal in the dark unless they have excellent local knowledge of the area or they are tugboat captains. I think what I saw—that boat and those two men aboard her—may have had something to do with the disappearance of the Calverts."

Again, strange indeed that Captain Morris was never interviewed by the authorities. There is no reference in over 600 pages of FOIA documents to this seemingly critical piece of information. Nothing at all

189

about an eye-witness sighting of a large boat with two males aboard in the middle of the very night the Calverts disappeared.

Chapter 52

Russian Exports

Fred Gerwing had loved his laughing, good-natured brother with all his heart. But, he knew there were a lot of questions before and after Dennis's death. "The investigators know I've been seeing someone" Dennis had told his brother. "I wouldn't tell them who it was because I know I'm going to be arrested," Dennis said.

Sergeant Viens wanted to know what kind of relationship Dennis had with a married couple, Laura and Rob Merrill, that lived on Hilton Head Island.

Fred replied he had been to social functions with the couple and that Dennis saw the woman, "a few times a week." He said she was a mail-order bride who was brought to the states to work in a strip club. He also thought she saw other men.

"I played golf with Dennis and dined with the couple and Dennis together. I thought the trio was 'sick,'" Fred said.

Fred said not only was he aware of the relationship between Laura Merrill and Dennis; he was somewhat aware of the financial agreement between them. He said the activity between the three became very volatile and he told Dennis, "You're playing with fire. If you don't think you are, you will be killed. The Russian Mafia will do it."

"I noticed a change in Dennis's tone around December 2007. He sounded like he was juggling a lot," Fred said, adding that he had talked to Dennis on March 5 after investigators met with his brother. "Dennis acted concerned during the conversation—about the financial situation, saying, 'There are financial problems to come,'" Fred said.

Asked about any connection Dennis had to strip clubs, Fred replied that he did not then know of any. He said he did know that Dennis had a relationship with the Merrills and that they had an import/export business that supplied used American cars to the Russian market.

He said he had learned that a large sum of money was paid to a company named Kazam Connex LLC that was owned by the husband, who bragged about being a Marine and in Special Forces.

"I saw one of the cars in 2007 in Dennis's garage," Fred said. "The cars were put on container ships and sent to Kazakhstan. On the other end, the wife's relatives collected the cars."

Fred said, "I mentioned this to Sergeant Viens, and I said, 'Why would you not put the Calvert's bodies in the trunk of one of these cars and ship them out of the country?' It was like she did not try to connect the dots. The police had to know there was more than one person involved." (So far as the authors were able to ascertain, authorities never followed the trail of the Kazam Connex shipments to Russia.)

"What else do you know about her (Laura Merrill)?" an investigator asked..

"Dennis was courting her (Laura) with a lavish lifestyle," Fred said.

Fred said Dennis took frequent trips to visit casinos. "Dennis made a trip to Louisville, KY to visit our dad, but never showed up at his house.

Instead, he spent his time at Caesar's Casino Riverboat," Fred said.

The bitterness Fred felt toward the Merrills continued after Dennis's death. "Rob contacted me and asked to come to Dennis's memorial service, and I told him that I did not believe that was appropriate."

Chapter 53

Follow The Money

One day, Fred Gerwing got a call from his brother Dennis who told him he was at the Atlantis Casino in the Bahamas. Fred later found several number charts in Dennis's home that he believed were flow charts that indicated an effort by Dennis to figure out how to beat the casinos.

"Dennis was obsessive/compulsive in some areas of his life," Fred, said. Asked about The Club Group losses, Fred said he had to assume they were a result of Dennis's gambling. Fred said he thought that was confined to casinos, that he had never heard Dennis speak of book-making nor had he known him to bet. He said he found no evidence of that in searching through Dennis's personal effects.

Dennis did, Fred said, invest heavily in the stock market—including one penny stock that went south on him. "Dennis took escrow accounts and was to put 2 percent into the stock market. He invested in different stocks, hoping to make more money and keep the profits. That did not work because most of the stocks he chose did not make any money," Fred said.

That assumption had credence in a report from FTI Consulting regarding the forensic audit of The Club Group. FTI identified a "secret" account at Liberty Savings Bank that Gerwing used to filter money through. He violated the management agreement between The Club Group and their clients, the audit said, by co-mingling their monies.

Dennis personally withdrew more than $1.5 million without the knowledge of his partner at The Club Group, Mark King. The move was accomplished by manually preparing transactions made by Dennis. The findings showed that The Club Group owed its clients approximately $2 million. Of the money personally obtained by Gerwing, operations revealed that the money went to Dennis Gerwing directly, then was distributed to the Merrill's company, Kazam Connex; the deported Russian dancer, Anya Bateava; the Mardi Gras restaurant owned by Louis Ross,; and Toddler University owned by Lesly Crick.

The audit said that during the first two months of 2008, Dennis prepared transactions to himself for $59,000, a transaction to *Big Girl*, LLC (his yacht) for $4,000, and a transaction to Toddler University for $22,000. The audit also found that a payment to the Harbour Town Slip Owners Association of $115,000 was not the full amount owed to them. Sheriff's Office notes said it believed that some of the money from the Slip Owners settlement was used to make the Calvert business whole.

Vien's report said, "It appears from the audit that was presented to me that a bulk of the money given to other individual/companies was paid to the export firm Kazam Connex, who received a total of $149,500 between 2007 and Dennis Gerwing's death. The Mardi Gras restaurant received $124,500 in 2007."

Fred Gerwing contended that after the audit the Calverts were missing only $55,000. "Dennis could have covered that so easily, in a heartbeat," he said. Fred said the total amount Dennis "moved" was $2.2 million.

Chapter 54

Lesly Crick & Toddler University

D ennis Gerwing and Lesly Crick were close. Fred Gerwing said that Dennis had given Lesly $22,000 to help her business.

The Freedom of Information Act obtained by the authors reveals that Lesly confirmed to the Beaufort County Sheriff's Office that she had a great affinity for Dennis. The FOIA records show the following:

"Dennis Gerwing and I had a close platonic relationship for nineteen years until his death. We met in 1989 when I started working for the Harbourside Café. Dennis was a fixture down in Harbour Town. He always hung out at the Harbourside or the Quarter Deck. He was a great employer and always made it a point to know all his employees,"

Lesly recalled Dennis with great fondness, saying, "He always had a big smile and a hug for you when he saw you coming. He was the sort of person that lit up the room when he came in. His laugh and big, boisterous voice made it known that he was 'in the house.' He was a big traveler and always returned with great stories and awesome pictures. He traveled with his girlfriend Nancy and their friends from Columbia."

Dennis was there for Lesly when she opened her business, and when she wanted to expand it. "Toddler University"—a licensed educational childcare provider that accommodated 86 children, was located at 22 Northridge Drive on Hilton Head. Lesly operated Toddler University for more than a decade and at one point wanted to branch out. She made plans and decided she would expand—at Pineland Station on US 278, the island's busy business route. She would need money and help.

"Dennis gave me business advice and helped with my payroll and accounting. Since Dennis's death, I have been racking my brain to figure out why someone so smart and so comfortable could take his life," she said

But, Lesly said she had noticed some changes in Dennis, "over the last few years."

In the FOIA, Lesly said, "At Hinoki one night a few years ago Dennis let me in on his little secret. He was seeing a married woman and had been seeing her for quite a while. Her name was Laura Merrill, and her husband's name was Rob. Laura had a daughter from a previous relationship, and Rob had a son from one of his previous marriages," she said.

"Was that one of the reasons you and Nancy split up?" she asked.

"That was part of it," Dennis replied

Lesly asked questions, and Dennis answered them. "He told me that she was a dancer he had met at the Gentleman's Club here on the island. He said he had been apprehensive to tell me about her, as he didn't want to ruin our friendship. I told him that we have always been great friends and I would never judge him. As long as he was happy, I was happy for him. We would talk about her and her husband. I didn't want to judge, but it was a very strange situation," Lesly said.

She didn't want to judge, but Lesly did express her concern. "I told him I thought the situation was bizarre at best. Rob knew that Dennis was seeing his wife intimately and supposedly supported it. Dennis and Laura would travel together, and Rob would fix them dinner when they returned like it was completely normal behavior. Rob would call Dennis to chat like they were great friends."

It was strange, thought Lesly, but she met them in Harbour Town during the Heritage Golf Tournament in 2005. "Dennis asked me not to tell anyone what she did for a living, so I introduced her as a friend and decorator from Savannah. I never told Dennis, but I didn't trust these people. I had a feeling about them, and I didn't really want to hang around with them. Rob was scary to me. He just seemed too slick. The only time we all spent an extended period of time together was on a trip to the Kentucky Derby."

To get there, Lesly said in statements obtained in the FOIA, "Dennis chartered a plane and took Rob, Laura and me to the Derby for the day. Rob seemed to know all about everything and anything. I really tried not to pay attention to what he was saying because he gave me the creeps. Something that did stick with me was his conversation about the things he did in the service. He said he was Special Forces and described how he used to kill people. I never understood why he felt propelled to tell us this except to puff himself up. It made me even more uncomfortable around him. I didn't think that trip would ever end."

Chapter 55

★

"I Didn't Like It"

Lesly Crick, to whom Gerwing had given $22,000, met often with Dennis. They enjoyed sushi and conversation. "We were having dinner at Hinoki, and the conversation got a little strange. He told me he was going to help the Merrill's start a business with Laura's uncle or father; I can't remember for sure. I asked a little about it," Lesly said.

"It's an export business where we buy old cars and send them to be sold over in Kazakhstan."

"That sounds a little risky, and what do you really know about her uncle or dad?" Lesly asked.

"I've researched it, and it looks like a good investment," Dennis said.

"I didn't like it," Lesly said. She said Laura "seemed to have some sort of spell over Dennis."

Then, discussion occurred between Lesly and Dennis about a restaurant in Savannah that had been opened by longtime Quarterdeck Restaurant and Bar manager and bartender Louis Ross:

"There were times over the last couple of years when we were doing payroll and then going out to Hinoki for sushi that Dennis would tell me about the mess Louis's restaurant had become. He had lent Louis Ross some money to help him get the restaurant started, and they were having all sorts of problems with staff.

"Around St. Patrick's Day, not long after the restaurant opened, there was an issue with the liquor license. Dennis was not at all happy. He had assumed the license was in Louis's name, but it was in the old manager's name, and she was not very cooperative with the license transfer. Dennis said the restaurant was struggling and he was doing what he could to help Louis. I assumed he was giving Louis money, but it wasn't something we talked about. The financial aspects of his investments and relationships were kept to himself," Lesly said.

Chapter 56

★

"Corporate Bitch"

What about John and Elizabeth Calvert? Did Dennis have problems with them?

Lesly Crick told investigators, "He said they wanted to end their business relationship. I asked what was going on."

Dennis replied, "It's a surprise to me, I had a good relationship with John and Liz. I told them after the sale of Harbour Town if they wanted to end the management contract all they had to do was let me know, and we'd do it in a friendly manner. I guess Liz didn't see it that way."

He added, "She's a serious corporate bitch!"

"He said Liz was accusing him of cooking the books. He said that he could account for just about every penny," Lesly said.

Just about? Standard accounting practices didn't use that phrase.

"John was basically a mediator in our meetings. Liz is the one who wears the pants in their relationship," Dennis told Lesly. "Dennis said he had been having meetings with the Calverts on a regular basis to go over accounts and, he said, "Most of them were stressful, at best," Lesly said.

She added, "Dennis always said, "Liz just didn't get it. He said Liz was, 'Going to do things her way.'"

Lesly's $22,000 loan—what about that?

On March 4 Coastal States Bank had asked for the company's financials, and Lesly turned to Dennis.

"He said he was going to get them (the financials) and we would gather more information from QuickBooks the next night when we did payroll. We had payroll and payroll taxes to work on before going to dinner Wednesday night, the 5th. Dennis was helping me by putting together a business plan and budget, along with financials to get an SBA loan," Lesly wrote in a statement to the Beaufort County Sheriff's Office.

"I had signed a lease in June of 2007 and was working on getting all the approvals needed for the center in Pineland Station. We were hoping to have everything done and move in by the beginning of January 2008. Things were not going as planned and approvals took longer than expected. I had been bugging Dennis to help me get all the paperwork into the bank but he was busy and time kept going by," Lesly wrote.

People needed to be paid.

Lesly was impatient with Dennis and said, "I kept telling him that I know children, not numbers. If I knew what to do with the bank, I would, but I'm clueless. I think I can max out my current SBA loan and pay the engineers and architects."

"Don't do that, it would look bad at the bank," Dennis said.

In January 2008 Dennis gave her a check to cover the amounts she owed.

"I can't accept that," she said.

Lesly had not, in 20 years of friendship with Dennis, asked for anything but his advice.

"Take the money," he insisted. "Use it to pay the engineer and architect, and when you get the SBA loan, we'll take a draw and pay it back."

She considered that and realized she was confident that Dennis would get all the loan documents together for the bank and she would be approved for the SBA loan shortly—she could pay him back quickly.

"That's the only reason I accepted it," Lesly said.

Dennis delivered the funds. She said Gerwing gave her $22,000. The amount was handwritten on a Club Group check.

Then, more delay in "getting the financials together."

"Every other Wednesday when we did payroll, I asked about getting the financials together, and he always said, 'don't worry, we'll get it done.' I was starting to get really stressed because I was supposed to start paying rent at Pineland, and there was no way I could pay rent in two places," Lesly remembered.

The stress mounted.

Chapter 57

"I Don't Know Who I Can Trust"

FOIA information indicates that Lesly Crick was fixated on meeting financial obligations: "Like I said earlier, we were supposed to get everything together on March 5, when we did payroll. Unfortunately, that never happened," Lesly lamented.

Dennis called her on a Wednesday night, March 5, around 5:30, to let her know something had come up and he wasn't going to be able to get together that night.

"He sounded funny, so I asked if everything was ok. He said he didn't know, but that he would call me later. I did payroll myself and went home. I guess it was around 9:30 or 10:00 that night Dennis called," she said, thinking back.

Dennis was upset. Liz and John Calvert had disappeared, and he had spent most of the evening talking with Beaufort County Sheriff's detectives.

"Why?" Lesly asked.

"Apparently John and Liz disappeared, and it looks suspicious. The detectives say I was the last person to see them. I asked what that meant, and he said no one had seen them since I met with them Monday evening," Dennis said.

"How did that meeting go?" she asked.

"Better than most of our latest meetings," Dennis replied.

Dennis added that the detectives had told him he was a person of interest, if not a suspect in their disappearance.

Lesly laughed at first because she considered it so crazy that they thought Dennis had anything to do with the Calvert's disappearance.

"Dennis couldn't hurt a fly," Lesly said.

"They probably just took off," she said to Dennis.

"John and Liz didn't say anything to me at the meeting about going on vacation or going back to Atlanta. I'm scared. Maybe you should come to the office tomorrow morning and pick up your financial binder. I'm afraid the Sheriff is going to freeze my accounts and do an investigation. I don't want you dragged into it," Dennis said.

"I asked him if he had done something wrong because he was acting guilty," Lesly said.

"No," Dennis replied, "but I truly feel if they want to find me guilty of anything, they will."

"Don't worry about anything—do you want me to give my friend Bob Bromage a call?" she asked.

"No, don't talk to anyone. I don't know who I can trust," Dennis said.

"I think you'd better get an attorney; they'll be able to guide you through this mess. I love you. Get some rest. I'll see you first thing in the morning," Lesly said.

Lesly went to The Club Group office the next morning around 8:00 to get her financials, about which Dennis had done nothing since September.

"He was visibly upset," she said of Dennis. Dennis told her he had gotten an attorney and was going to meet with him at 9:00 that morning, before talking again with detectives.

"I want you to distance yourself from me," Dennis said.

"We were both crying," Lesly said.

"You are my best friend, and there is no way I'm going to leave you alone at a time like this," she said, through her tears.

"You have to," Dennis said, crying.

Dennis told her, Lesly said, that after their talk on Wednesday night, he had gone to see Laura and Rob—to say goodbye to them.

"What do you mean?" she asked, fearful.

"I don't think I'm going to see any of you again. I think I'm going to be arrested this afternoon," Dennis answered.

Dennis made a phone call to Columbia to tell Nancy Barry the same thing. He let her know she should get her things together and move out.

Dennis, Lesly said, was very scared.

"Why are you acting so guilty and scared?" she kept asking Dennis.

"If they want me guilty then they will find me guilty! Liz has been accusing me of taking money. I can account for all but about $15,000 which is part of what they owed me," Dennis said.

Lesly hugged him and said, "I love you. Stay calm. Call me after you meet with the detectives."

Dennis did so, calling her that night around 8:30.

"He sounded much better than he had that morning, he seemed more relaxed," she said.

"How did everything go?"

"Well, I'm not in jail."

They laughed, and Dennis said, "They weren't happy about the attorney. They took my cell phone."

Dennis then asked her about Detective Bob Bromage.

"My attorney said it might be a good idea to talk with him," he said.

Lesly knew Bromage would be at a mutual friend's birthday party the coming Saturday and she might have the opportunity to talk to him informally.

"You need to get out and relax with friends," she said to Dennis.

"That sounds good; I'll talk with you Friday."

Chapter 58

"When It Rains, It Pours"

Saturday morning, March 8, 2008 Dennis called Lesly.

"He said he needed to go to Columbia to help get the house ready for an open house Nancy and he were having. I told him I understood. Late that evening he called me and said he was getting ready to leave for Columbia when he got word that 'they' had search warrants for his house and cars. He said he was going to take the keys to them and he was going to stay with Dan Duryea that night. I was happy to hear he was going to be with a friend and not alone," she said.

"Do you want me to come with you?"

"No."

"I'll talk with Bob when I see him this evening," she said.

But, that was not to be. Bromage left the party at their mutual friend's home before Lesly could chat with him.

Dennis called Lesly Sunday morning, March 9. "He called from his house. He was pretty upset because his house had been turned upside down during the search. He sounded defeated," she said.

"Are you ok?" she asked.

"Yes, I'll be fine."

"Did they find anything?"

"No, there was nothing to find. I'm going to try to clean up, and I'm going to stay with Dan again."

"You should just have someone come on Monday to clean and enjoy the day," Lesly said.

"Thanks, I'll give you a call tomorrow."

Lesly called Dennis Monday at his office to ask what she needed for the bank. The people at Pineland Station were getting antsy, and her contractor wanted more money to start building.

"I know I shouldn't have burdened him with my issues, but I was truly thinking that he was getting back to a normal routine. He was very stressed and a little short with me," Lesly said.

He was indeed short. Dennis said, "Well, when it rains, it pours. I need to go. The office is a disaster. I'll call you. We'll get together tomorrow."

"That was the last time I spoke to him. I started getting phone calls from friends around 5:30 Tuesday evening, telling me that Dennis was dead. I was in complete shock. I was tired of hearing rumors, so I called Mark King, and he confirmed that Dennis was dead. It was a shock then and is still a shock to me today because I know Dennis, and he would never kill himself. I know he did, but there is too much mystery around the whole suicide and Calvert disappearance," Lesly said.

FOIA information shows that Lesly finished her heartfelt and anguished statement by saying, "I don't trust the Merrills or anyone involved with them. I feel like they are involved with everything. I don't know if any of this will help, and I will try to remember anything of importance and pass it along. The more I look back; I really believe that Dennis kept things vague for my protection."

Chapter 59

★

Dogs & Cats

As rumors about the Calverts swirled around Hilton Head Island like a series of nasty gales hitting Calibogue Sound, life went on. Marina employee Laura Tipton called an Atlanta kennel every few days to check on John and Liz's black 45-pound mixed breed dog, Sadie. Laura and other Calvert employees also walked daily to the *Yellow Jacket* to feed the Calvert's cat, TC.

They spent some time on the yacht, waiting for TC to eat so they could gather him up in their arms to stroke and soothe him. They knew TC had an eye infection and they tenderly applied eye drops they had found in the boat's cabin. They felt TC was just waiting for Mom and Dad to return, shouting endearments to him as they boarded their home on the water.

Hilton Head Island was known as a haven for animals and, online, the islanders began to prove their reputation for the love of their pets was solid:

"I thought I read that their dog was in a kennel, does anyone remember that? If so, I wonder if that was the usual practice even for a day?"

"That was my understanding as well. I'm not sure that anything has been said about the accommodations for the dog. It was mentioned that the cat lives on board the boat."

"The best that I could find was that the dog was at a kennel in Atlanta where they have their other home. Not positive about that though. So maybe when they stay on board the boat the dog goes to a kennel."

"Heard on the news that a person of interest who had last seen them had been found dead from suicide. I hope they're sure it is suicide."

Laura Tipton called around to see if she could find out if anyone she knew had any information about her missing employers who were her good friends. She knew there were others such as she—people who loved the Calverts.

"I talked to one of their oldest, dearest friends, and he was saying they never wanted to move to Tahiti or something like that. Hilton Head was their dream. They were living their dream," Laura said.

Meantime, Liz's brother David White worked diligently to keep the Calvert businesses functioning. On March 22 David told reporters Brownstein and Donnelly, "All the employees are hanging in there. Everyone's been very accommodating for the last three weeks."

Tony Gibbus, the manager of the Mariner's Club and a friend of the Calverts, told the reporters that John Calvert had a system that allowed his managers to run his businesses when he was not around.

White said, "We are very close to getting salaries paid and very close to getting money for all the operations. The bottom line is: They are functioning. They will function much better next week, and they will all be paid."

Chapter 60

Issues Unresolved

For Dennis Gerwing, the Hilton Head Island dream had turned sour.

"It all happened at SPC," Dennis had written in his suicide note. "It," according to Michael J. Prodan, the SLED criminal investigative profiler, referred specifically to the Calvert's murder. "SPC," he said, was shorthand for Sea Pines Center where The Club Group offices were located—the last place the Calverts were seen.

On October 22, 2009, DeKalb County, GA Probate Judge Jeryl Debra Rosh ruled that John and Elizabeth Calvert were dead. In the declaration, the judge said a Beaufort County Sheriff's Officer report, "Seems to indicate an admission," by Gerwing that he killed the Calverts. The report concluded that Gerwing's motive for killing himself, "was his fear that the public would find out about his embezzlement of funds from his clients."

The judge's ruling listed several reasons that seem to rule out the urban myth that the Calverts were alive and might be in a federal witness protection program or on some Caribbean island. It was noted that a reward of $65,000 had generated no information about the Calverts' fate or whereabouts and that the Calverts did not fit the profile of those who became missing persons. And, the order said, the Calverts had not used their cell phones, and they had not accessed their credit cards or used an ATM since the time of their disappearance. The judicial order said, "The Sheriff's Department has both of the Calverts' passports so that international travel would be difficult."

Indeed, there had been no sightings of the Calverts even though the FBI continued its search, and Interpol maintained a "Yellow Notice" watch in 150 countries—Case Number 20080715863. Further, the United States Marshall's Service had 186 cooperating countries monitoring any attempt by the Calverts, if they were still alive, to leave or enter any of those countries.

All that certainly seemed to put to rest the possibility that the Calverts were alive. They were dead—officially.

And yet, the Calvert case remained of intense interest. It was, after all, the most sensational event ever to occur on Hilton Head Island, and many contended John and Elizabeth were still alive—somewhere.

Did Dennis Gerwing commit suicide? Dennis, his neighbors and friends said, was the most unlikely person they could think of who may have contemplated taking his own life.

"I think there are a lot of issues here that are unresolved, and (there are) a lot of people here in the public who have a lot of questions that don't add up, if you know Dennis like I did," Dick Sonberg, Gerwing's neighbor of 15 years, told media. Sonberg said Gerwing never seemed depressed even in tough times when he lost money on business ventures or had medical problems.

Sonberg said Dennis enjoyed wine, but wasn't a hard drinker and wasn't into any other substance abuse. "He was always up and going," he said. Gerwing's friend Frank Fowler was quoted as saying, "In my heart of hearts, I just would find it very difficult even to conceive that Dennis would be involved in anything that was not above board."

Chapter 61

★

"A Hitter's Gun"

Roger Franklin, writing in the April 2011 Hilton Head publication, *Posh Island Rail* speculated, "hard looks at the circumstances surrounding the disappearance of the Calverts leave few realistic opportunities for the inarguable unobserved snatch. While it was undisputed that Gerwing was the Calvert's last known contact, that was never substantiated."

Franklin continued, "Regardless, while the BCSO summary still has Dennis Gerwing acting alone, a time-defying and physical impossibility, it points to the probability that a third party successfully executed a well-laid plan to isolate, subdue, contain and murder the Calverts, then take their bodies off the island unobserved. It was flawless." (Franklin's reference to the Calvert bodies being taken off the island "unobserved" points to the importance of Captain Ray Morris's sighting of a mysterious boat at the Harbour Town Yacht Basin the night the Calverts disappeared.)

Franklin went on to say that an assassination of the Calverts would have had to have Gerwing's cooperation to murder them. He speculated that the third party, or parties, also had planned for Gerwing to take the fall. Franklin contended that Islanders believed the murder was a professional hit by a high-dollar professional organization.

How did someone dispose of the bodies? The Club Group offices were located on the second floor of Sea Pines Center. Most who gave thought to the matter believed Gerwing shot both John and Elizabeth with his .22 Beretta—a caliber noted for a small entrance and little blood flow.

The .22 Beretta was the definitive pocket pistol. It weighed just 11.5 ounces and was easily concealed. Its snag-free lines allowed it to be tucked into any holster or a pocket. Manufacturers described it as user-friendly and durable. Further, it was extremely accurate. Jamming and stove-piping problems were virtually eliminated by an open slide design. It was called a "hitters gun" and would do considerable damage if an assailant shot a victim in the head. The bullets would ricochet inside the cranium, but minimal external bleeding would occur.

Think of it. If Dennis did it, how did he do it? Did he walk behind John and shoot him in the head first, before Elizabeth arrived? Then, did he pull the small pistol out of his pocket and shoot Elizabeth in the back of the head? Or, did he pull the Beretta from the desk and shoot each of them point blank in cold blood—one after the other. Did they resist in any way?

There was additional speculation and conjecture—what if it happened as follows?

Dennis hit the down button of the elevator outside The Club Group and waited. He fished in his pocket for the keys to John Calvert's Mercedes— keys he had retrieved a few minutes earlier from the trouser pocket of a lifeless form on the floor of his office.

Dennis hurried down the stairs of Sea Pines Center and ran to John Calvert's silver Mercedes. He nervously looked around and then unlocked the door of the vehicle. Dennis slid under the wheel and drew the safety belt across his ample midsection. He hit the ignition and quickly drove out of Sea Pines Center.

Thoughts raced through his head. What had he done? Why had he done it? Was he doomed? Where could he stash the car?

Driving out of Sea Pines Plantation, he swung the Mercedes through Sea Pines Circle and exited on US Business 278—the William Hilton Parkway. He just drove, seeking a place to leave the Mercedes, a place where he could easily get a ride back to his office and two dead bodies.

Intersections and traffic lights came and went as perspiration oozed onto Dennis's brow, his head turning to look into every parking lot, trying to determine where to dump the car. Then—to his right, the perfect place. He turned off US 278 into the swank Palmetto Dunes Plantation and headed toward the Marriott Resort and Spa.

Dennis drove into the hotel parking lot and directed the luxury automobile toward the first available space. Empty coffee cups on the front passenger seat jiggled as the car jerked to a stop. Dennis opened the car door, swung both legs to the pavement, and heaved himself out of the car. He slammed the door, took one last look at the Mercedes, and turned toward the hotel entrance.

Sweating profusely, he hurriedly walked to the front doors of the hotel and waited for the airport shuttle to the airport where he picked up his Toyota Avalon. There would be no record of his coming or going. He took the Avalon to Sea Pines Center and parked in the parking lot in back of the center where it was seen on Truffles camera. He then walked back to the front of the center and drove Liz Calvert's Mini Cooper to the Liberty Oak parking lot in Harbour Town and walked back to Sea Pines Center.

Dennis then took his Yukon to CVS for Band-Aids and rubber gloves and stopped for fuel before returning to Sea Pines Center.

Dennis returned to his office and knowing what had transpired, donned latex gloves and, gloved hands shaking, went about the gruesome business

221

of wrapping two dead bodies in drop cloths, binding and securing them with tape or rope—strands of a rope that would be later found in his Avalon. He then checked to make sure the 2nd-floor area, which contained 9:00-5:00 businesses, and a late closing restaurant, was deserted.

But, the above imagined scenario leaves out speculation that Dennis *did not* kill the Calverts—someone else did. Was it possible an accomplice, or accomplices, shot and killed them? Did the Calverts meet with, not only Dennis, but with others, in Gerwing's office, unaware that a .22 bullet was about to end their lives? If they did, would they have known the other people Dennis had invited to the meeting?

Chapter 62

★

"Weak As Water"

The question continues to this day—did Dennis act alone?

There were many theories—and the conjecture goes on—what if it happened this way:

The 5'8" Gerwing pushed open the door of The Club Group and dragged the first body through it. He muscled the heavy burden across to the elevator and pushed the "down" button. His heart pounded as the doors opened, revealing an empty compartment. Dennis shoved and pulled the dead weight onto the elevator.

Or, was a second party helping him drag the body? Could one person heft all that dead weight?

Imagine:

The doors opened on the first floor, featuring shops and restaurants. The last business to close at night at "SPC" was Truffles Café. It closed its doors at 10:00 pm. There was no one in sight. Dennis pulled the dead body from the elevator out to the loading dock of Sea Pines Center. There, Dennis—or his accomplices—had pulled his vehicle up to the dock. With adrenaline pumping, Dennis alone—or with help— pushed, lifted, and slid a lifeless form into the vehicle.

Sweat growing under his armpits, Dennis brushed his hair across a wet forehead and slammed and locked the vehicle. He turned and retraced his steps to the elevator and the murder scene in his office where he began the movement of the second body.

Could Dennis have done all that himself—out of shape, overweight, not known to have substantial physical assets—a person said to be timid?

Was there video surveillance?

Yes, there was surveillance video on equipment at Calibogue Café & Trading Company (the space later occupied by Lowcountry Produce). It was of Dennis outside the restaurant the night of March 3—the night he met with the Calverts and the evening they disappeared. That video shows Gerwing alone, nervously pacing back and forth around 6:40 pm.

Other cameras in Sea Pines—at Truffles Café and Forsythe Jewelers in Sea Pines Center and at the Sea Pines Plantation security gate—produced video with such low resolution, authorities said, that they were of no value.

There was, however, clear video of a white male (authorities called the man a "white male" but it is patently clear they believed the man to be Dennis Gerwing) pacing back and forth just outside Calibogue Café & Trading Company the early evening of March 3, 2008, at various times, from 6:40:53 pm through 6:49:26 pm.

The surveillance camera, investigators wrote, "located at the center counter island just inside the front door of the restaurant. The camera is six (6) minutes slower than real time. This camera is directed toward the front door and looks outside into the center of the courtyard of the Sea Pines Center. The left side of the camera frame is toward the front parking area of the Sea Pines Center. During the course of the video a white male walks back and forth across the frame just outside the restaurant. The white male appears to be wearing a yellow colored short sleeve shirt and dark colored long pants. The profile, age, and clothing of the male appears to match Dennis Gerwing and the same clothing that he is seen wearing earlier in the evening by Ryan Alpaugh, and seen on surveillance video from CVS Pharmacy and Station One Shell Station."

Dennis was again recorded there, at various times, from 8:36:04 pm until 8:59:04 pm, March 3, 2008, and a third time, in the same location, from 11:02:37 pm through 12:50:30 am March 4.

He is last recorded at that location at 1:19 am March 4, 2008.

At one time, investigator notes said, he was seen talking on a cell phone. At another time he was seen carrying a square case with a shoulder strap, noted in investigative reports as possibly a laptop computer case.

The FOIA references a security camera at a bank (now closed) at Sea Pines Center located near where Dennis was said to always park his vehicle. But the authors could find no indication video footage was obtained and reviewed from that camera. That is considered important in that Dennis's vehicle might have been in an area observable by a camera at the bank location.

It was noted that a Truffles Café camera did show clear video at one point in the early morning hours of March 4, 2008. A BCSO report of July 27, 2008 says: "The video collected from Truffles Café documented a sedan leaving the back side of Sea Pines Center in the early morning hours of 03-04-08."

What else could have happened?

Dennis could have driven his vehicle almost to the elevator at the

Sea Pines Center from a ramp on the east side of the complex. This would allow him to more easily load the bodies.

What did Sheriff Tanner think?

"There's no evidence to suggest anything different (than Gerwing was the assailant)," Tanner told media. "Different people have had different opinions of Dennis Gerwing. You have those who say he was weak as water. Both John and Liz Calvert were not large people. Then you've got others who say he was very capable of doing it. He had a very hot temper.

"Physically, it wouldn't be any problem doing it. Dennis was pumped up. There was a point in time during the encounter when he was enraged," Tanner said. He added, "People are capable of doing lots of things in those type of situations. Based on people we interviewed, he was very capable of doing it."

On December 10, 2008, at a news conference, Sheriff Tanner described Gerwing as over-extended financially and about to be exposed for embezzling $2.1 million from the Calverts and seven other clients. "It appears Dennis is responsible for the disappearance," Tanner said.

But—there appeared to be hesitation, as Tanner added, "Right now we have him acting alone, not associated with anyone else, but that's something we're still looking at."

In the same meeting with the media, Tanner said, "At this stage, it's going to be difficult to get anyone to come forward. This is a very closely shielded case. The problem is that if anyone has information about this case, they could very likely be a co-conspirator or co-defendant."

Chapter 63

"There May Be Another Layer Of This Story"

"We thought there was a part of the story missing," *Island Packet* reporter Dan Brownstein told the authors in 2017. "There were fundamental issues about the apparent suicide and the Calverts disappearances and suspected murders. Dennis killed himself in a very gruesome manner. He seemed to work up to it—wounding himself and trying to figure out how to do it. It would be challenging for someone else to be involved, and, at face value, I think he killed himself."

Brownstein paused, and then went on. "But things pop out. I tend to think Gerwing had stolen money and probably knew what had happened to the Calverts and some underlying criminal activity. It seems unlikely one person could kill two people, get out of the building and do so in a way that there is no forensic evidence. It seems to me a very unlikely scenario. Here's this pudgy guy who did not fit the bill that he could cleanly kill and remove two people from the building. He was not a hardened criminal," Brownstein said.

"How did he get them out of there with no trace?" fellow reporter Tim Donnelly asked. "How did he dispose of the bodies? Even if he dumped them in a gator pond, how did one man do it? There were tarps; gloves were bought, it's hard to believe he was the only person involved."

The two also said they thought it strange that The Club Group, through public relations executive Tom Gardo, at one point released a statement acknowledging that there was some money missing and that Dennis had embezzled it and then, almost immediately, Gardo tried to retract the statement. "That was strange," Brownstein said, "we wrote a whole article on that."

"Another question—people said the Calverts were in a witness protection program and they asked if the Calverts were clean in this case. I can't say 100 percent either way. They were straight laced, but you just don't know. Maybe they are gone because they want to be gone. Something shady?

"My impression is that the story went much deeper than Dennis, and serious embezzlement and money laundering might yet be uncovered. There could be a connection to organized crime. We never saw any evidence of a shadowy Hilton Head mob, but there may be another layer of this story that has not been revealed," Brownstein said.

The two reporters were in unison that, from what they had seen, not much new evidence was revealed since they were working the Calvert story, "It went cold pretty fast after Dennis killed himself," Brownstein said.

Chapter 64

"A 700 Pound Roll Of Hay"

There were those who believed, most assuredly, that Dennis Gerwing was assisted in transporting and loading the Calverts' bodies in his vehicle—after all, disposal of the bodies would have been tough if he acted alone.

Where to put two bodies? Closest and perhaps easiest would be, of course, the Sea Pines Plantation lagoons. Throw the bodies in there, and the alligators would dispose of them in no time. Or, perhaps not—and if the alligators did not consume all of a corpse, body parts would surely have been found if the lagoons were drained.

What about burial in the Sea Pines Forest Preserve? Not likely a natural pursuit for Dennis, even if he had help—and cadaver dogs would surely find a fresh gravesite.

Perhaps that led Dennis to ferry the Calvert's bodies to the Harbour Town Yacht Basin and a waiting boat—a boat that Captain Ray Morris saw mysteriously docked at the Harbour Town fuel dock, almost hidden in the dark.

Again, acting alone, or with the help of the two crewmen from the boat in Harbour Town. Dennis would be dragging two cord-tied tarps containing bodies down the gangplank and onto the boat in Harbour Town. Did the investigation cover every area where the bodies might have been dumped? Consider the fact that Dennis Gerwing was there on videotape as he drove through the exit of the Cross Island Parkway toward Squire Pope Road. He did not reappear on the Parkway surveillance video for five hours.

Could Dennis have been headed toward Savannah when he passed through the toll booth, heading west? The five-hour gap would have given him time to drive, at night, the 45 minutes to properties managed by The Club Group in Savannah, do some business and return.

What kind of business? Well, some speculate, Dennis may have decided to dispose of the Calverts in a private lagoon in a deserted area of one of the Savannah properties to which Dennis had Club Group access. Did he have help? He would have had to wrangle the bodies into the lagoon alone, not a small task. But, once the labor-intensive effort was by the boards, the alligators would have done the rest, hungrily disposing of the evidence.

Then—what about the commercial grade drop cloths? Would Dennis have had to unwrap the bodies for the alligators to get to the remains? Wherever the drop cloths are, the designation as "commercial grade",would probably guarantee the thick material did not decompose.

"Why wasn't the Savannah disposal possibility considered?" is a question still asked on Hilton Head. Dennis did have a sense of humor. Could he have gotten a "last laugh" by disposing of the Calverts' bodies in a lagoon at "Mystery Valley"?

Mystery Valley, after all, was a development managed by—The Club Group.

Sheriff Tanner agreed there were lots of unanswered questions and he told the media it was frustrating to run into dead ends, likening the investigation to finding a needle in a 700-pound roll of hay.

All of Hilton Head Island waited—hoping something would break in the Calvert case.

Then, in October, 2011, that hope seemed to turn to reality. The FBI in Columbia, SC forwarded to the Beaufort County Sheriff's Office an anonymous letter with a Los Angeles, CA postmark. The envelope contained a satellite photo and GPS coordinates of an old hunting club in the woods of nearby Eastover, SC in Richland County. The Calverts' remains, the letter said, could be found there. Further information would be forthcoming, the letter writer stated.

Investigators, aided by archaeologists from the University of South Carolina, rushed to the scene. They unpacked their gear and began an intensive inch-by-inch search for remains or graves. Undoubtedly, the Calvert destiny would be revealed on that day.

Nothing was found.

"We felt that was the break we had been looking for," Sheriff Tanner said. "It was frustrating when we found nothing." The additional information the letter had promised was never received.

There is a postscript:

In 2017 interviews by the authors, as this book was being written, one associate of Dennis's, Jerry Burden, who worked for The Club Group, and who left in the 1990s to work for another firm, commented that Dennis had a day trading operation in his office where sums as high as $100,000 a day were traded by Dennis. Burden also said that when he left The Club Group the accounting balanced and showed no discrepancies.

Jerry said he and Dennis were driving back to Hilton Head one day from a trip to Savannah to look at computers. They crossed the Savannah National Wildlife Refuge that covers 15,000 acres in South Carolina and 14,000 in Georgia. It is where endangered alligators that became too friendly with humans were transported, enabling them to grow into very large specimens. It is designated as the "Savannah National Wildlife Refuge" because its water runs to the Savannah River.

As Dennis and Jerry were driving past dozens of large alligators sunning themselves on the banks of the lagoons on Alligator Alley, Dennis remarked, "If you ever had to get rid of a body, this would be the place."

Many areas of the refuge are extremely remote. So far as the authors know, no search was made of the area.

Chapter 65

★

Chardonnay

Theories—many theories.

Dennis Gerwing did not commit suidice—he was murdered. Many islanders believe this without a doubt. And who could blame them? The bathroom where Gerwing's body was found had blood practically pouring under the locked door. No fingerprints were found on the serrated kitchen knife that was found next to Gerwing's body.

What about the almost empty wine bottle and the wine glass downstairs at Dennis's villa? The Sheriff's Office told the authors it was not possible to tell if the wine bottle was a red or white container, only that it was a cheap wine. However, zooming in on official pictures taken of the wine bottle, the word "Chardonnay" was plainly printed on the label on the backside of the bottle. The brand? Kendall Jackson—not world-class expensive, but hardly Mad Dog 20-20. Dennis drank only red wine, and had no alcohol in his system, according to the coroner's report. Who drank the Chardonnay? Was there any effort to obtain DNA from the glass?

It was a Mob hit, others say. Gerwing embezzled, by some accounts, more than $2.1 million. How could he have stolen that much money over many years without being discovered? What happened to all that money? Gerwing's lifestyle was full of gambling, girls, high-cost purchases—but, even so, $2.1 million?

Did mobsters demand Dennis embezzle from the Calverts to pay his gambling debts? And did the mob then assist Dennis in rubbing out John and Elizabeth? Or, did Dennis begin to shift more of the money to his account, rather than share and share alike with co-conspirators? Was money-laundering going on?

Speculation was rampant, and the Internet went wild. Blogs were posted carrying all sorts of scenarios. One posted comment read:

"I guess that Gerwing was the mastermind, using the Calvert company to launder—remember—lots of cash came into a big, fancy, top-notch marina legitimately. That gives you lots of ability to clean up dirty money. Something tells me that the Calverts did not take a boat out to sea and meet up with a round-the-world cruise ship and sail off into the moonrise."

The post continued, and the writer said:

"Gerwing was relatively new, and could change accounting and bookkeeping to hide laundering money for quite some time."

One has to assume the writer meant Gerwing was fairly new to the Calvert accounts.

The post went on:

"However, whoever set this up did not count on a transactional business law-yer figuring it out. They obviously thought she was little Miss Rich Hilton Head/Savannah housewife whose goal in life was the next fancy party and spending money. Gerwing decided to skim a little or misled his conspirators as to what the Calverts knew. The Calverts got fed to the fish because they ran the place and perhaps were ignorant or had just discovered what was going down. Gerwing died the way he did because that's how the Colum-

bians and Jamaicans do business when double-crossed."

Another post said,
"Look, if it ain't money, it's drugs. A boat goes out every weekend for a spin in the ocean and a little charter fishing. The fishing for fish stops and the fishing for little floating garbage bags begins. Boats keep coming in and out, and no one is suspicious until perhaps they notice the boat keeps taking the same guys out fishing and they don't look like fishermen if you know what I mean.

"If the Calverts were eliminated, 'cause they really did not know what was going on in their business and the crooks needed to remove a law abiding obstacle, and Gerwing was stealing, or perhaps hiding money, looking for a better deal, this ALL makes a TON of sense. Gerwing murdering the Calverts and then, when the law closes in, killing himself in the way that he did, makes zero sense."

The post concluded:

"This is South Carolina; he could have gone to a pawn shop and left with a gun the same day. No need to try to kill himself with a serrated steak knife. Heck, he could have wired money to the Bahamas and taken a charter out of Hilton Head before Tanner even suspected."

Online, "Anonymous" said:

"Vacation rentals are somewhat seasonal, and money could be laundered by falsely filling in rental dates during slow periods, paid for of course. Maintenance costs could be padded as well. Marina charges could be inflated to launder more money. Somebody gets greedy and sloppy.

"The heat is on, and the operation may have been under investigation. Two of the players either get to [sic] close to the truth or were involved all along and under scrutiny. They are 'disappeared', kidnapped, possibly killed, or swept off in the dark of the night into the Witness Protection Program (which I doubt would be told to local authorities). One of the players ends up dead carved up like Christmas turkey, either by his hand or someone

235

else's. Perhaps by yet unknown players who feel slighted."

Anonymous continued:
"There seems to be a greater effort than we normally see in this area when someone comes up missing. That would lead one to think that this is a special case for some reason or another. It appears that this is deeper and more complicated than the typical case of this type. That would certainly explain the limited release of information. If it turns out to be a large tentacle beast, the authorities would make sure not to compromise the case with too much information."

"No, wait," some islanders said, "there is no doubt—Dennis murdered and disposed of the Calverts all by himself!"

Others ground their teeth and said, "How could Dennis alone have carted two dead-weight bodies out of the office, down the elevator, into the Yukon, and then dumped them somewhere? He had to have had help!"

And, remember, island coffee klatches heard time and time again, no one knows how Dennis's Toyota was moved from the Hilton Head airport to his home in Hilton Head Plantation—or how John Calvert's Mercedes found its way to the Marriott parking lot in Palmetto Dunes.

Not only that but—what about that theory that John and Elizabeth are in a witness protection program or on some far-flung distant island, sipping umbrella drinks? Sheriff Tanner and a judge's ruling both say that's nonsense. The Calvert banking accounts and passports remain untouched. Their cell phones have never been activated, and their cat was left behind.

Did the Calverts find a final resting place somewhere in Calibogue Sound or farther out in the Atlantic where the sharks are plentiful? What were the means of conveyance? Gerwing's boat was being repaired in Charleston and the Calvert yacht, so far as anyone knows, was never moved from the Harbour Town Yacht Basin from the time the Calverts disappeared.

There is another possibility, of course—don't forget Captain Ray Morris's account of a mysterious boat at the Harbour Town fuel dock in darkness the night the Calvert's disappeared. Captain Ray wonders if it had something to do with the mysterious disappearance of two high profile Hilton Head entrepreneurs—but there is no record the authors could find that authorities were aware of that sighting.

Or—are the bodies buried somewhere? There were, after all, those muddy boots, a shovel, and, in a home that was otherwise extremely tidy, a pile of dirt on Dennis's kitchen floor.

Detective Bob Bromage would leave no pile of dirt untouched—he had the soil analyzed by state crime labs, hoping it might provide clues that could help narrow the area where the Calverts remains might be buried. The soil in Beaufort County was, after all, different from that found elsewhere in the Palmetto State. But, no report has been found on that soil analysis.

Chapter 66

Tarps & Latex Gloves Discovered

On December 12, 2008, Detective Bob Bromage contacted Mark King's wife, Leslie King, at Club Group Realty. Leslie had listed Dennis Gerwing's home in Hilton Head Plantation for sale after Dennis's death.

She added an interesting footnote to the case when she told Bromage that she was cleaning out Gerwing's home "a few weeks ago," just before a "walk-through" by the buyer of the property. There, she told Bromage, she found two tarps and a box of latex gloves.

She told Bromage she disposed of the items because the residence was being sold. Leslie said when she saw a media release of December 10, 2008, and read where Gerwing had purchased similar items on the date of the Calvert's disappearance, she felt that they may have been the items not recovered by law enforcement.

Bromage asked Leslie to come to his office where he showed her photographs of the drop cloths similar to the one purchased by Gerwing. Bromage's report said that King advised him the items in the pictures he showed her were not the same as the tarps she found in

Gerwing's residence;

King was asked to follow Bromage to the CVS where Gerwing bought the latex gloves. After viewing the boxes of gloves on the shelves that were similar to what Gerwing had purchased, King advised Bromage that the latex gloves she found in Gerwing's home were not CVS brand and said she could not recall what the actual brand name was.

King was asked to prepare a statement. She did so, sending it by email at 1:40 pm on December 15, 2008, saying in a statement within the FOIA obtained by the authors:

"Bob,This is just to confirm that the plastic covers that could be in-terpreted as 'drop cloths' that I observed at Dennis Gerwing's home were, in fact, in completely different packaging from the pictures you showed me today in your office. The two packages I observed were packaged in sealed and unopened clear plastic bags, with little or no printing of any manufacturer's nor brand name.

"One package had a light blue plastic 'cover' inside a clear plastic bag., folded in about a 9" x 12" or probably, more-square, like 12" x 12". They were quite heavy, altho' not bulky. The other package was exactly the same size except for the plastic inside the clear plastic package was a clear plastic color.

"These were originally located on a shelf in one of the guest bedroom closets, and we later moved all the contents in the closets out to the shelves in the garage. They remained there until just last week or the week before when we cleaned out the house for the final walk-thru for the buyer.

"2) The small box of latex gloves was yellow in color with red print but I didn't recognize the brand name—it was something I had never heard of, but resem"

At that point, the Sheriff's Office's stamped certification of the email document obliterates the few words in the rest of the sentence—the

240

email picks up on the next page.

"bag box, with perforated top which, was opened, and the box was practically full of gloves. It was located in a cupboard below the sink in the laundry room off the garage, in plain sight when you opened the doors of the cupboard. I have a vague recollection of Nancy or someone in her cleaning group either having the gloves on or mentioning that she would leave all the supplies (and possibly the gloves?) for the final cleaning. All of the boxes we observed at CVS appeared to be in CVS generic packaging of blue and white colors and were completely different in size and color than the ones found in the laundry cupboard.

"I'm glad we were able to clarify the differences. Please let me know if you have any other questions." Leslie.

Strange, looking at the email ten years later—why weren't the drop cloths and gloves discovered in the original search of Gerwing's home? Were they placed there later?

And, if so, by whom? Leslie's email seems to suggest the cleaning crew may have put them there. Was the cleaning crew ever interviewed?

Chapter 67

★

Mystery Cruise

Tom Barton, Editorial Page Editor of the *Savannah Morning News*, wrote of the September 7, 2008 "Mystery Cruise" off Hilton Head Island that contained, "A boatload of questions still hoping for answers." His report captured a moment in time loaded with pathos.

Barton wrote, "They laughed about the old days and shed tears over the new ones." The boat contained 80 or so friends, relatives and business associates of John and Elizabeth Calvert. They were aboard the *Spirit of Harbour Town* on a Sunday evening, setting sail from the Yacht Basin in the shadow of the Harbour Town Lighthouse.

They had all journeyed dockside to help raise money for the reward fund for John and Elizabeth. But, more than that, Barton wrote, "The unstated purpose was more complicated: To remember two well-liked people who enjoyed life—and to wish them what could be the last farewell."

One passenger told Barton, "It's probably the closest thing to a wake we're going to get." The passenger sobbed as Barton noted, "a fat orange sun dipped below the horizon and painted the sky over

Calibogue Sound in vivid violets and pinks."

Barton wrote, "It was a gorgeous sight, one of many that lured mon-eyed people to this resort island and its famously laidback lifestyle. It helped hook the Calverts, who had all but relocated here from Atlanta."

David White was aboard the *Spirit of Harbour Town* that night. He told Barton. "We don't know anything more than what the media has been told. It's extremely frustrating."

Barton's column said, "And for a good reason. The Beaufort County Sheriff's Department doesn't appear to be closer to cracking this case than it was back in March when the couple vanished. And the trail gets colder each day."

Barton commented, "Unfortunately, the dead make lousy witnesses. They also can't defend themselves."

Barton said. "His scissor hands-style death has been ruled a sui-cide—a finding that no one I talked to on this cruise believes."

The Savannah editor reported that there was some talk on the boat about using a $62,000 reward fund, $17,000 of which was raised that night, to hire a private investigator. "Normally," Barton wrote, "you hate to spend down an account that might entice someone to squeal. Informants will sing arias if the price is right. But given continued silence and apparent lack of progress by Sheriff P.J. Tanner on this six-month-old case, hiring a P.I. looks like money well-spent."

Barton spoke with Nancy Calvert, John Calvert's aunt and one of his few living relatives. She had traveled to Hilton Head from Fairfax, VA for the cruise. "While dining at an island restaurant, she overheard strangers talking about her nephew and his wife and their probable demise, and how their remains could be anywhere—even at the bottom of the lagoon outside."

Barton said John's aunt asked to be moved to another table. "I would, too," Barton said.

Barton closed his account of the Mystery Cruise as follows: "Words, however, don't cause the deepest sting. Worse is the fear that someone might get away with a horrible crime against two good people. But before there can be justice, there must be answers. Friends hope that ship hasn't sailed."

Chapter 68

"Turning Them Over To God"

October 22, 2009, DeKalb County, GA, probate court Judge Jeryl Debra Rosh declared John and Elizabeth Calvert dead. Rosh's law clerk, Mark Brandenburg, said the court had jurisdiction in the case because the Calverts were legal residents of DeKalb County. David White breathed a sigh of relief. "I believe the hearing that declared them deceased does move us closer to some sense of closure. Turning them over to God will also help," he told the *Savannah Morning News*.

The judge's order alleged that Dennis Gerwing had embezzled not hundreds of thousands of dollars, not $2 million, but, this reference insisted, $4 million from Calvert accounts, and the accounts of others Gerwing served.

The Calverts were dead—or so a judicial decision said.

On November 15, 2009, at 2:00 pm, at Northside United Methodist Church in Atlanta, more than a year and a half after the disappearance of John and Elizabeth Calvert, a public memorial service took place. Elizabeth's brother, David White, said before the service that he hoped the gathering would help the family, and the community, honor his sister and her husband.

White had quit his advertising job in Atlanta and had taken over the Calvert's businesses on Hilton Head. He said he assumed those duties, "So they can walk in and take over. It's hard, but I'm doing this for Elizabeth and John."

White set up the reward for information regarding the whereabouts or deaths of the Calverts, and it ultimately reached $65,000. No information on the Calverts disappearance came forward, and no reward would be given. The money that was raised was diverted to underwrite Calvert scholarships to benefit Converse College, where Elizabeth received her undergraduate degree, and John's Georgia Tech fraternity, Beta Theta Pi. David White said John and Elizabeth would be pleased the money would be used to help others.

David managed the Calvert's businesses until February of 2011 when Sea Pines Resort purchased them. The price was not disclosed. Included in the transaction were the Calvert company managerial and operational functions. Those responsibilities covered fishing services, yacht services, fuel sales, water sports and sightseeing cruises.

Sea Pines president Steve Birdwell said Sea Pines bought the business to deal with boaters and customers directly. Birdwell said the company would keep the Calvert employees.

Bill Barnett, mayor of Spartanburg, SC, who served on the Board of Trustees at Converse College with Elizabeth Calvert, said he thought there was a sense of closure at the memorial service—but, "Whether it's a slam-dunk guaranteed 'end' of the story, I'm not sure."

Hundreds of people from Beaufort County, Atlanta and Spartanburg, attended the service. Converse College president Betsy Fleming, befriended Liz when Betsy was interviewed at Converse. Fleming said, "There was a wonderful crowd. I think that they were two individuals who were greatly loved by many." Fleming had admired Elizabeth's forthright manner when Liz grilled her during her interview for the

College presidency, pressing her as to her plans to, "Shake up the status quo at the college."

The service was, Fleming said, "A wonderful celebration of each as an individual and them as a couple." She mentioned their talents, their gifts, how much their lives meant to other people, how much they gave of themselves in terms of humor, and personality. We expect Liz and John to live on for generations."

Chapter 69

The Search Continues

Ten years after the disappearance of John and Elizabeth Calvert a complex and intriguing mystery remains. Family and friends have waited for ten years for their questions to be answered and no answers have been given.

The Beaufort County Sheriff's Office refused to close the case, but it was a case they had not solved in a decade. And prospects for future answers appeared to be dim. On June 12, 2008, Detective Bob Bromage wrote in a Supplemental Incident Report, "An investigation has yet to reveal their whereabouts."

Bromage's report said:

"I spoke with (Staff Sergeant Angela) Viens, and it was learned that SLED was unable to develop a DNA profile of John Calvert on his personal items previously submitted. I then contacted Nancy Cappelmann (custodian of Calvert's yacht) and requested access to the Calvert's yacht located in Sea Pines Plantation.

"Cappelmann advised that she was in possession of the key to Calvert's yacht and agreed to meet with me at 10:30 am on 06-10-2008. Upon meeting with Cappelmann, she contacted David White (Elizabeth Calvert's brother), and he was advised of the necessity of collecting additional items for a DNA profile. Collected from the Calvert's yacht were the following items.

1. Brown boat shoes
2. Norelco electric razor
3. Men's grooming kit with case
4. Eye glasses with case

Note (by Bromage) The above-listed items are believed to be the personal items of John Calvert. Nancy Cappelmann secured the yacht upon completion of the collection of the items.

Disposition of Evidence.

"I turned the items collected from the Calvert's yacht into the BCSO Evidence "

Division on 06-10-2008 at 1:47 pm. A SLED form requesting DNA analysis on the items was completed and accompanied the evidence.

"Attachment- BCSO Evidence Submittal Form."

SLED had failed to obtain DNA—Bromage was determined to have it—but even this effort failed to provide DNA results.

The Calvert case dragged on, and it was so frustrating that Sheriff P.J. Tanner even lent an ear to former law enforcement retirees who lived in nearby Sun City who had, on their own, decided to review the Calvert case. They asked to meet with Tanner. To the surprise of some, the Sheriff agreed.

The retired enthusiasts called themselves the "Lowcountry Retired Law Enforcement Officers Association," consisting of retired police officers, investigators, and attorneys. They invited Sheriff Tanner to come to the retirement mecca of Sun City, perched near Okatie, SC, halfway between Bluffton and the access to Interstate 95 south to Florida, or north to Columbia, SC.

Tanner not only accepted the invitation; he listened intently when the seniors asked him how they could help.

Tanner did not hesitate to take their offer seriously, and he looked over the membership roster. He studied credentials and then selected participants from the enthusiastic group and gave them the sobriquet, "The Cold Case Review Team."

The missing Calverts had become a community obsession. John Varone, the Sun City volunteer group vice president, told media, "It's too cold to fish. Hunting season is over. Why not?"

And Sheriff Tanner is still on the hunt. He said many times that no one had been identified throughout the investigation as a second party to Dennis Gerwing.

Tanner conceded to a reporter the possibility of another party's involvement, especially since it would help explain Gerwing's untraceable movements on the day and night of March 3, and further resolve how John Calvert's car ended up at the Marriott Resort at Palmetto Dunes.

"Cab services and taxis in Hilton Head didn't pick anyone up. That would lead anyone to believe that there was a second party, which very well could be. You just hope someone with some loyalty to Dennis Gerwing at some point will decide, 'OK, well, he's dead,'" Tanner said.

Tanner told *Unresolved Mysteries*, "My feeling has always been (the Calverts) are three, four, five hours from here because there is an 11-hour window where Dennis Gerwing's phone is powered off, and we couldn't find him."

Chapter 70

Many Loved Him

Was Dennis Gerwing a bad guy? Well, there is abundant evidence that he seemed to fit the definition of the old saying, "Sometimes bad things happen to good people." Or at least one would think that of Dennis while reading guest book condolences posted online by Dunbar Funeral Home in Columbia SC on December 12, 2008:

"I worked with Dennis frequently when we both worked for Arthur Andersen in Denver. He was a great guy, a good supervisor, and an all-around wonderful person. I will miss him!
-Donna Weeden

"Dennis will live on thru [sic] both of you. He was a wonderful person, and it was a pleasure to know him and to be proud of him. Think only of the good times and the wonderful memories."
-Teresa Mathews

"My deepest sympathies to Dennis' family. I worked with Dennis at Arthur Andersen in Denver and always thought so much of him. I remember him always smiling and enjoyed seeing him at the last Alumni reunion."
-Jean Burns

"Fred and Beth, you are both in my thoughts and prayers. I never met Dennis, but I do remember Fred's stories that were always told with a smile and a glowing face. Everything happens for a reason. God will get you through this. I miss you guys. Hang in there.
-Anita Finley

"My deepest sympathy and condolences go out to Dennis' family and friends. I will always remember the fun times we had back in high school and college and consider myself very lucky to have known Dennis and to have him as a friend."
-Charlie Aubrey

"I had the joy of knowing Dennis for eight short years through Nancy. He opened his home and his heart to me. I will miss that great laugh and hearing stories of his worldly travels. There is a new star shining brightly in the sky. Dennis—you will be missed but never forgotten."
-Jean Mobley

"Dearest Uncle Dennis, we will all miss you so much but are so grateful for all the wonderful memories. Love, Lauren and all your nieces and nephews."
-Lauren Stern

"I, too, am a friend from Dennis' days at Arthur Andersen in Denver. Dennis lived life with joy and pizazz. A group of us went to Hawaii in the early 80's, helped by Dennis' resort association. We had a blast, and that trip will always be a special part of my memories of Dennis. My heart goes out to his father, siblings and nieces, and nephews. I will be praying for you and remembering the fun, kind and gracious Dennis Gerwing we all knew. Love, Dawne."
-Dawne Murray

"As Fred stated so well, boy you knew how to live your (-) Dash!! We will all miss your generosity, kindness, friendship, and especially your laugh!!! I know you, and Mary Helen are pacing as you watch us from above."
-Tammy Duryea and Family

"We are so sorry to hear of Dennis' passing. We enjoyed many good times with him and Nancy in our supper club together several years back. He never met a stranger. Our hearts are with you, your family and especially Nancy."
-Beth and Duncan Watson

"We love and miss you, Uncle Dennis. We will never forget you. Love always, Jules."
-Julie Payne

Chapter 71

★

Life Goes On

The Calvert's bodies may or may not be on Hilton Head—but, in a beautiful and tranquil area of Sea Pines Plantation, there is a reminder that John and Elizabeth were once vibrant names on the barrier island that called to them.

In Six Oaks Cemetery, beneath tall and stately oak trees, is a tribute to the missing couple that Hilton Head Island cannot forget.

There, just off Greenwood Drive in the gated community of seaside dwellers, a lone marble bench has been placed. It is engraved with two names—John and Liz Calvert.

The smooth, shiny bench, where one can rest and contemplate, is a poignant memorial that speaks of two people who, by most accounts, led good lives.

TC, the Calvert cat, now lives with a charter operator and his family.

The Calvert dog, Sadie, also lives with a new family.

Liz's brother, David White, sold the 40-foot Hatteras Calvert yacht, *Yellow Jacket* in 2009. He remained on Hilton Head, engaged in the management of former Calvert businesses until he sold them to Sea Pines Resorts.

Gerwing's yacht *Big Girl* was lost in foreclosure.

P.J. Tanner remains Sheriff of Beaufort County, SC.

Detective Bob Bromage and Lieutenant Angela Viens remain with the Beaufort County Sheriff's Office.

Island Packet Reporter Tim Donnelly moved on to *Inc. Magazine, The New York Post, Brokelyn Magazine,* a webmag about living big on small change in Brooklyn, NY and is now a researcher for *The Presidents Show* on *Comedy Central* in NYC.

Packet Reporter Daniel Brownstein moved from reporting to Communications Director for the Fourteenth Circuit Solicitor's Office, working for Solicitor Duffie Stone; he then became a freelance writer and from there became Director of Marketing and Communications for Richardson, Patrick, Westbrook & Brickham, LLC in Mount Pleasant, SC.

The Crazy Crab and Red Fish, favorite haunts of the Calverts and Gerwing, continue to do a flourishing business on Hilton Head Island, SC.

Attorneys Chuck Scarminach, Dan Saxon, Peter Strauss and Cory Fleming continue to practice law on Hilton Head Island.

Captains Peter Ovens and Ray Morris sail the Calibogue Sound and the Intracoastal Waterway.

Mark King continues as CEO and the driving force of The Club Group.

Nancy Berry continues to live in Columbia with her dachshund Heidi, named for Dennis's dearly departed dachshund Heidi.

There was never a search of the house in Columbia after the Calverts' disappearance.

Dennis gave Nancy a $30,000 life insurance policy on his life in the case of his death. The insurance company did not want to pay Nancy. Insurance agent John Carswell stepped in and insisted she be paid. The company relented, and paid Nancy. Nancy said, "It helped me reconstruct my life."

Captain Toby McSwain left the Beaufort County Sheriff's Office to accept the position of Chief of Security at Sea Pines Plantation.

Lesly Crick remains on Hilton Head Island.

The Sun City Cold Case Review Team is still attempting to solve the Calvert mystery.

Sheriff Tanner hopes to solve the Calvert mystery.

The Calvert Cold Case file remains open.

Timeline

2005
★   John and Elizabeth Calvert purchase businesses on Hilton Head Island

2008
Monday, March 3
★   Dennis and his assistant Sha Ha drop off his Toyota Avalon at private airport parking lot on HHI

★   At 4:20 pm Dennis buys 3 drop cloths at Grayco on the way back from airport

★   At 4:45 pm Elizabeth Calvert's friend Teri McClure cautions Liz to meet Gerwing in public…Liz is not concerned

★   At 5:30 pm John Calvert is seen by Chris Lobello on the stairs on way to Dennis's office

★   At 5:32 pm Liz is east bound at toll booth on the island

★   At 5:40 pm Liz is seen boarding her yacht Yellow Jacket

★   Around 6:15 pm Liz arrives at Dennis's office

★   John & Liz are never seen again

★   6:40 pm to 6:49 pm Dennis is on video pacing back and forth at Sea Pines Center

★   At 7:26 pm Dennis buys Band-Aids and latex gloves at CVS

★   At 7:30 pm Dennis drives through west bound toll booth

★   At 7:40 pm Dennis buys fuel for his Yukon

Tuesday, March 4
★   Early morning, Avalon seen leaving Sea Pines Center

★   Captain Ray Morris sees mysterious boat at Harbour Town

★   Dennis takes Yukon in for service and takes taxi back to Sea Pines Center showing up around 1:00 pm

★   Investigators interview Dennis at The Club Group offices and later that day at his home

★   Missing Person reports filed for Calverts

Wednesday, March 5

★   Dennis's assistant, Sha Ha, picks Dennis up at his home noticing his Avalon was back at his home then takes him to pick up his Yukon from service

★   Police search the Calvert's yacht *Yellow Jacket*

★   Sheriff's Office considers but does not name Gerwing as a Person of Interest

★   Calverts officially listed as missing

Thursday, March 6

★   Dennis Gerwing tells Nancy Cappelmann he may have been the last person known to see the Calverts alive

★   Dennis engages an attorney

★   Sheriff takes Dennis's cell phone.

★   FBI and Sled join the case with the Beaufort County Sheriff's Office

★   Dennis has dinner with friend, Dan Duryea

Friday, March 7

★   At 2.21 am John Calvert's Mercedes found at Marriott Resort in Palmetto Dunes and searched

★   Dennis at Red Fish with a "tear in his eye"

★   Dennis visits Albaughs at Calibogue Café & Trading Company in Sea Pines Center

Saturday, March 8

★   Dennis tells Nancy Barry a search was issued for his home, office and cars and took his cell phone

★   Dive teams search lagoons and creeks

★   Detective Bromage interviews Mark King

Sunday, March 9

★   Frank Fowler and Gerwing exchange emails

★   Dennis spends night at Dan Duryea's

Monday, March 10
★   Attorney Scarminach asks Dennis to come in next day to sign papers
★   South Carolina Law Enforcement Division (SLED) adds agents to assist in the investigation
★   Sheriff's Office interviews Dennis's assistant, Sha Ha
★   Dennis spends night at Dan Duryea's

Tuesday, March 11
★   Detectives again interview Mark King with Bob Long and George Murray
★   Dennis is named as a Person of Interest (he dies before being notified)
★   Saxon, Strauss, King and Long go to Swallowtail, call 911
★   Firemen arrive at Swallowtail Villas in Sea Pines
★   Sheriff's Office arrives and discovers Dennis's body in bath room
★   Candlelight Vigil in Harbour Town for the Calverts

Wednesday, March 12
★   Gerwing's death officially ruled a suicide

Thursday, March 14
★   A Russian informant appears

Saturday, March 16
★   Cadaver dogs join searches

Thursday, March 27
★   "Motivational Suicide" term introduced

Thursday, June 12
★   Investigation has yet to reveal Calvert's whereabouts

Wednesday, December 10
★   Leslie King called Detective Bromage about items she finds at Dennis's home

Friday, December 12
★   Lesly Crick reports to Sheriff's office regarding a Beretta
★   Atlanta Funeral home posts remembrances

Monday, December 15
★   Leslie King provides statement to Sheriff's Office

2009
★   Calvert's yacht, *Yellow Jacket* sold

April
★   Mark King assumes full responsibility to pay back those Dennis swindled with Fred Gerwing's help

2010
Tuesday, May 4
★   Sheriff P.J. Tanner opened the Beaufort County DNA Lab which allowed evidence to be processed in a timely man ner without waiting for SLED'S lab, the second one in the state

2011
February
★   Liz Calvert's brother, David White, sells Calvert businesses to Sea Pines Resorts

Saturday, October 22
★   Calverts declared legally dead

Tuesday, November 15
★   Memorial service for the Calverts in Atlanta

2017
Wednesday, September 6
★   10:00 am Authors interview Tanner, Bromage, and Viens

Deceit, Disappearance & Death
on Hilton Head Island

Colophon

The text is typeset in Berkeley Old Style Book.
Frederic W. Goudy was one of America's most prolific
designers of metal type. He worked under the influence
of the Arts & Crafts movement.
It was either 1938 or 1940 that Frederic W. Goudy created the
first Berkeley typeface that falls in the classification of the old style
serif font category. Goudy designed the font for the University
of Berkeley and the design became the beginning of the Berkeley
typeface history. When it was first released, it was called the
"Californian" font.
We chose this font because of its off-center look that suggests
something is amiss which we deem fitting for this book.
The cover photograph is by William L. Bosley and
the cover design is by Pamela Martin Ovens.
The book has been printed by ArtBookPrinting.com
a specialty markets company of InnerWorkings, Inc. in the
United States of America.

Acknowledgements

Our thanks to Beaufort County Sheriff P.J. Tanner, Detective Bob Bromage (now Captain) and Detective Angela Viens (now Lieutenant) for their interest in our endeavor and the time they spent with us as we researched this book.

Thanks also to The Club Group CEO Mark King for his assistance in developing the timeline of the iterations of Sea Pines Plantation ownership and development of his company.

Fred Gerwing was very generous with his time and knowledge and contributed a great deal to this book.

Chuck Scarminach and Dan Saxon of Novit & Scarminach; Rick Peterson, owner of the RedFish Restaurant; Nancy Barry of Columbia, SC; Frank Fowler; president of the Harbour Town Slip Owners Association; former *Island Packet* reporters Tim Donnelly and Daniel Brownstein; and Captain Ray Morris all provided detailed recollections that added greatly to this accounting.

The authors thank Captain Peter Ovens whose diligent collection of articles and personal remembrances relating to the Calvert case, and his encyclopedic knowledge of Hilton Head Island and its residents, past and present, made this book possible.

Grateful appreciation is extended to editors Becky Ryan, and Beverly and Ivar Samuelson who spent many hours reviewing grammar and sequence within the book.

About the Authors

Charlie Ryan and Pamela Martin Ovens previously collaborated on *The Pullman Hilton, A Christmas Mystery* and *My Life with Charles Fraser,* chronicling the recollections of the men and women who worked for and knew Fraser, the iconic founder of Sea Pines Plantation.

Charlie Ryan was, over a span of eighteen years, a radio and television news director and anchor, Associated Press state broadcast editor and newspaper columnist. His reportorial years were spent in West Virginia and St. Louis. In his journalism career he focused on politics and interviewed notables including Lyndon Johnson, Richard Nixon, Eleanor Roosevelt and Robert Kennedy. He is a recipient of numerous honors and a member of the West Virginia Broadcasting Hall of Fame.

Following his broadcast career, Charlie founded and grew four media firms in West Virginia, Virginia and Washington DC. After 35 years he sold the firms and became the founding dean of the Graduate School of Business at the University of Charleston in Charleston, WV.

Charlie and his wife Becky moved to Hilton Head Island where he served three years on the board of directors of the Sea Pines Plantation Community Services Association as chairman and the Association of Property Owners. They now reside in Charlotte, NC.

Charlie has also written *Dead Men's Clubs* and *Alacrity*, his memoir.

Pamela Martin Ovens has lived on Hilton Head Island for almost 40 years. She and her husband, legendary boat captain Peter Ovens, are widely known from their charter sailboat business of 16 years, hosting hundreds of tourists on the 62-foot yacht *Schooner Welcome*. Pamela is the chief executive and owner of Single Star publishers. She was a radio and television professional in Cincinnati prior to her move to Hilton Head Island and hosted an island radio show on WHHR. Today she is an accomplished "voice over artist" for radio and television commercials.

Index

A

B

N

O

P

R